A Thin Place

where two worlds meet

by Gordon Smith

First published in Great Britain in 2016
Cove House Publishing Ltd, Cove House, Shore Road, Cove, Argyll G84 0NP

This paperback edition first published in 2016

ISBN
978-0-9935818-1-6

Printed in Great Britain by William Anderson & Sons Ltd, Glasgow

First Edition

www.covehousepublishing.com

Dedications

To Princess Meg, my very own Bramble - for all the love and joy she gave so unconditionally throughout her life.
To Ileen Maisel, my friend and someone who pushed me to write this book and whose vision may take it into another dimension.
A special dedication to all the people I have worked with over the years to help understand and work through their grief; may you all be filled with light.

Acknowledgements

To Lizzie Henry, once again I owe a debt of gratitude for your excellent work on editing this book.
To Lynn Cleal and Andrew Smith for helping to bring the book to life and allowing it a place on the bookshelf.
To Robbie Ringwood for always being there to keep things right when I lost sight of things.
A great big thanks to my two sense speaking friends, Cookie and Lizzie for letting me walk them through our own Dip-n-Dells and feel the power of nature at its best.

MAY ALL BEINGS BE HAPPY

Contents

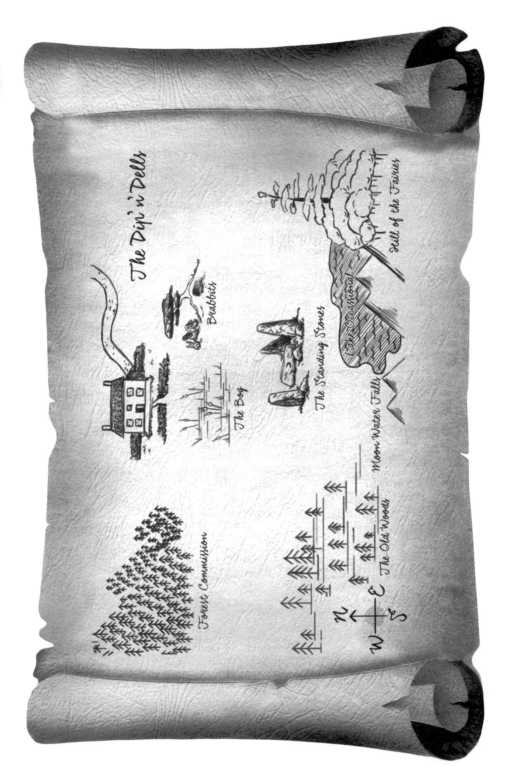

The Dip'n'Dells

Hill of the Fairies

Brabbits

The Standing Stones

The Bog

Moon Water Falls

Fort Occasional

Forest Commission

The Old Woods

Prologue

'No parent should ever have to watch their child die!' Mrs Thornberry barked out loudly to the cold empty kitchen.

Shouting out made her feel that she was fighting back in her emotional battle, somehow stopping the sadness and anger from taking root in her body.

As the words rebounded in echoes across the space, she screamed, 'Oh, this is so unfair!'

She dropped forwards to lean on the solid wooden table in front of her, aware that her arms were supporting more than her body weight; it felt as though a huge boulder was resting on her shoulders.

Tears streamed from her eyes. She knew that she had to expel these emotions when they built up in her; she was trying so hard to be strong.

'Someone has to be strong in all of this,' she said in a more sedate tone to the empty fireplace on the other side of the room.

She stood up straight and threw back her head, pushed back some long strands of wiry grey hair that had come loose from the stack bundled on the top of her head, and headed for the back door. She needed to breathe in some fresh country air to remind herself of why she was here.

Emerging from a narrow dark wooden porch, she straightened her body to its full height, wiped her eyes with the back of her hands and breathed in the warm clear air from the endless space all about her. She knew the importance of letting go of these painful emotions, but she had to be strong to help her daughter and her family just now; after all, they were the ones who needed support. It was they who had lost a child, her granddaughter, Amber, who had recently died of cancer. She had to prepare this old cottage for them.

Taking in her surroundings, from the rundown garden to the green expanse that stretched before her, she stopped thinking altogether for a moment and stood completely still, at one with this country paradise. For so much of her young life it had been a safe haven, a place where she had found healing and tranquillity, a place that was now filled with magical memories. This was why she was bringing her family here: to find peace and to fix their broken lives after the terrible tragedy they had just been through.

The remaining child, her grandson, came into her mind. He was so young, only ten years old. He needed to be cared for and given an understanding of what was really going on. Grief had taken his parents from him; her hope was that this magical place would be the key to their return.

She had total control of her emotions now, and a new-found strength began to enter her body, moving up through her feet as if the ground itself was charging her with energy. It felt as though a burst of strength and compassion had entered her being, and she knew that these were just two of the elements she required for the work that lay ahead of her.

She wanted to stay here longer and allow all the good memories of her own childhood to flood back into her mind, but she fought against it. She was aware of how powerful this place was, but it wasn't for her this time. No, everything it could give would be for her daughter and son-in-law – they had had so much emotional weight to bear in the past few years.

Turning her head slowly, she took one final look around the landscape, taking in the most obvious sight, which was a large hill with tall trees on the top reaching up to the blue sky. For a moment she seemed to be looking at something happening in the space above it, and a smile broke over her face. She thought of her grandson, half-shut her eyes and made a wish. She wished that he would be touched by the same magic as she had been when she was growing up in this beautiful place.

Then she disappeared back through the small wooden porch and into the old cottage.

It was time. Something had begun.

Chapter One

A Dark Time

Dill was standing in the overgrown garden at the back of his new home. The garden was as wild as the countryside that surrounded it; in fact, other than a small stone wall, which was half-buried under moss, ivy and ferns, there was no real way to distinguish where the garden ended and the vast expanse of wild scenery began. It was a chilly October day and he was thinking about his sister, who had died the previous summer, and wondering where she was now. Did a part of her still exist somewhere, and if so, where? He felt sad inside.

Darkness had entered his life since she left.

'No, it came before, didn't it?'

He blushed with embarrassment as he realised he'd spoken out loud to himself again. He wasn't exactly sure when this had started, but he was certain that it had only been since he'd come to the new house. That was a week ago now. But the darkness had been there before. He called it that because it made him scared at night when he was alone in his room.

'But that was in the old place, wasn't it?'

He'd done it again. Or had he? Something strange was definitely happening to him.

His mind was pulled back to the bad dreams he'd had in his old house and how alone he'd felt. He felt the same now, even when his mum and dad were with him. It seemed so long since they'd all laughed together. His parents had been sad even before Amber had passed away and Dill had felt it whenever he'd been with them. But the sadness was different from the scary darkness – there was something more threatening about that.

Only when Dill was with his old grandma did he gain any relief from the heavy feelings that hung over his family. Grandma had a way of talking that made him feel at ease with everything. Maybe he felt this simply because she did speak to him, even about Amber's death. As far as he could remember, neither of his parents had talked to him about it, not afterwards anyway. They had told him it was going to happen and then there had been silence. He wondered why as he stared ahead of him into a rugged wilderness.

A dot appeared in the distance. It seemed to disappear and reappear every few seconds, moving in and out of the mass of heather, bracken and gorse that covered the rolling landscape all the way to a wooded area. Soon it was getting bigger and closer and was moving erratically from side to side in a way that was almost hypnotic to watch. Dill smiled as it began to form into a shape: that of his big old floppy, bouncy, liver and white springer spaniel, Bramble, someone else who made him feel good.

Dill had wanted Bramble to play with him in the garden, but every morning since they'd been in their new home the dog had shot out of the door and dashed off into the wild terrain, where she'd played for hours before staggering back with her head drooping and her steamy tongue hanging almost all the way down to the ground.

But today Bramble seemed to know that Dill needed her; it was almost as if they could talk to each other from a distance in a language that needed no words. He always knew either just before she wanted to go out or when she was coming home; he knew when she was hungry and when she wanted to play. And in return she seemed to know when he was afraid at night or when he felt sad, and she would slap big kisses all over his face or sit up on her back legs to make him giggle.

In fact Dill had noticed that lately the dog was more attached to him than ever before; she had begun to show him more affection and had started to sleep by his bed. When his parents had gone to bed, she would even get into bed with him and snuggle tightly into his body until he fell asleep to the gentle rhythm of her breathing. It was as if she was standing guard for him, making sure that no scary darkness could enter his room.

He turned to look at the house for a moment and noticed that even though the sun was shining all around it on this crisp autumn morning, it seemed to be covered by a cloud. It reminded him that inside the cottage everything was dark. Even his parents seemed to be covered in a dusty grey powder. It had begun to form around them just before his sister had gone into hospital for the last time.

'Is that when the darkness came?' he said to himself in a low whisper which turned to vapour as it left his lips and was picked up and carried off by the cool breeze.

He wanted to think more about this, but his attention was caught by Bramble, who was making high-pitched yelping sounds and tearing off in a new direction, as if on the trail of an animal or bird. Dill knew this sound and it made him laugh. He could tell exactly what his dog was feeling at this moment and she was very happy.

Another thing he'd noticed about her was that she was the only one in the house who had light around her. Ever since Dill could remember he'd seen light around people and animals, and Bramble was always shining brightly, even when his parents were very dark and sad. Since they had come to their new home this had become even more apparent.

The dog disappeared from his sight now and his mind dropped back into memories of when his parents had told him that his sister had gone to heaven. They had told him that she was with his grandpa and she was very happy there and she was in a beautiful place of light with angels and God. They'd made it sound amazing, but it didn't add up, Dill reckoned, because they'd still looked as though they were in pain. And it seemed as if she'd taken some of their light with her. He wondered if she'd had to use it to get into heaven. Maybe she'd send it back somehow.

He really hoped that the light would come back to his parents, because even though they didn't speak much these days, he could tell what they were thinking and feeling in the same way as he could with the dog. When his mother smiled at him and told him how happy she was about moving to their new home, he felt that other words were being spoken from a place deep inside her. Words like 'joy' and 'fun' were coming out of her mouth, but her gut was saying 'guilt', 'regret', 'anger' and 'loss'. It didn't make sense.

The same thing was happening with his father, too: he kept talking about being brave and strong and yet Dill could hear sobs inside him, and they seemed to be there all the time these days, even when his father played games with him and read to him and threw sticks for Bramble. It made him wonder about this heaven place. He knew that what his parents were telling him wasn't the truth, and he was angry about it, but then he remembered how sad they were and felt guilty for being cross with them. He also wondered why he could hear and feel things now that he couldn't before, and how it was possible to think so many things at once. Sometimes it felt as if his head would burst.

Just in time Bramble arrived with a dramatic leap over the stone wall, proudly showing off the spoils of her adventure: a disgustingly smelly stick, which she must have dragged out of the boggy patch just yards from the garden.

She held it up for Dill to take an end and play with her, but it was so smelly that he ran away, calling out, 'No way, keep away, smelly dog with that disgusting stick!'

This just made her chase him round in circles, waving her stinky prize in the air, which caused a slimy green substance to fly in all directions.

'Brams, I meant it!'

Dill began to giggle and then laugh out loud, and the dog replied with low, playful growling sounds which, if he read them right, meant that she was very happy at the response she'd got from her friend.

Dill knew that Bramble would never be allowed in the house with that trophy, and also because the entire lower half of her body was covered in the same slime as the disgusting stick. Yet even though almost all of the white parts of her body were covered in dark slime, she still had a bright white glow around her.

Dill gazed down at her as she lay on a patch of grass, bathing in what little warmth there was on this chilly day and panting so hard that white puffs of steam were coming off her long tongue. Once again he heard her silent laughter and began to laugh out loud himself as he fell to his knees beside her. Instantly she rolled over, asking for her mucky tummy to be rubbed, but there was no way he was ever going put his hand near her filthy underside.

His mother opened the kitchen window: 'Time for lunch, Dill, and don't let that filthy animal anywhere near my clean kitchen floor.'

He always felt sorry when Bramble had to remain outdoors while he ate, but a warm slurp of big wet spaniel tongue on the side of his face told him that she didn't mind. Besides, she had lots of work to do pulling her scabby old stick to pieces.

The kitchen seemed dark and a heaviness filled the room in spite of the warm fire that was burning in the fireplace. Dill loved the open fires in this new house and the sound of wood crackling always made him feel at peace.

Lunch was on the big wooden table, which meant that he had to sit on a cushion on a heavy wooden chair to reach it. He was quite small for his age, though he remembered being told how grown-up he was becoming by his grandma three weeks ago, on his birthday. He had felt happy that day because it had been the first time his parents had had light around them in ever such a long time.

He suddenly realised that he missed his grandma. She had always stayed with him when his parents had had to take his sister to the hospital. Grandma always had light around her and he could never remember hearing hidden words when she spoke to him. Her words were always straightforward and always made him feel good and safe and protected. As he looked down at his plate, he thought of her and wondered when she would come to stay with them. She had promised she would.

His mother was looking very tired, her eyes were red around the edges again and she was smiling one of the smiles that made her look very sad. Even though she made no sound, he could hear sobs and dull muffled whispers from somewhere in the depth of her stomach. As she pushed her hair back from her face, he noticed how little was left of her nails. He tried to remember when she had started to bite them.

There was an awkward moment of silence that seemed to hold them both in freeze-frame.

Suddenly she broke it by saying, 'Dillan, I want you to eat all your lunch before you go back out to the garden. The food will give you warmth and make you strong. It's getting cold outside, too, and I want you to wrap up. Oh, and don't let that dog jump up on you – she is filthy and will have to be bathed before she comes indoors.'

Dill found it hard to take in all the words, as his mind was still on pause, so instead he just nodded and began to eat the warm bowl of vegetable soup that was in front of him. He took one of the two pieces of bread that accompanied it and put it in his pocket, as he knew that Bramble would want something to eat too.

'She must be cold,' he thought, 'and she needs food to give her strength and warmth as well.'

Footsteps were coming from the room above, which his father used as an office. It was where he did all his work now. Dill didn't really know what he did as a job, but it involved a big computer and lots of talking on the telephone. He'd been told that his father wouldn't have to go out to work when they moved to the new house, but he hadn't realised he'd see less of him than when they lived in the old place. Not that he'd spent that much time with him then, as he'd had to go away on work trips a lot as well as the trips he'd made with his mother and sister. Dill had hoped that in this house he'd be able to play with his father more, but instead he'd retreated into his office.

Even Bramble missed going for walks with him. She'd get so excited when he lifted her lead and whistled for her. Dill always loved the scene she would make: she would spin round and round on the same spot, making it difficult for his father to attach the lead to her collar, and when she eventually did sit like a good girl, her bum would wriggle on the floor. Then she would fluff out her long furry ears. Just remembering it made Dill feel happy.

Lunch was over now and he couldn't wait to get back out with the dog. She was waiting for him because she knew that he had a treat for her in his pocket. Bramble could find anything, especially when it came to food, and Dill wasn't even fully out of the back door when she snatched the chunk of bread from his pocket and swallowed it in one gulp.

As soon as Dill entered the garden, he felt better. The heaviness that entered his stomach when he went indoors would leave the moment he stepped out of the door, especially when he was with his dog.

They played for a long time at Bramble's favourite game, which was chasing her old tennis ball. No matter how far Dill threw it or how deep it went into the bushes and ferns around the garden, she would always emerge with it in her mouth and run back to him with it, her head in the air and her small docked tail wagging to show just how clever she was.

The days seemed to last longer in this place and the only way Dill realised it was becoming night-time was when the sun changed from a bright ball of yellow light into an even bigger ball of soft pink or sometimes orange or red light, which always happened when it was over the small trees to the right of the house and just before it began to sink out of sight behind them.

In the daytime it seemed to sit on the highest hill in sight, the one that had all the trees at the top of it, which lay to the left of the back garden. Dill liked looking at that hill, and even more so when it looked as though the sun was touching the very high tree at the top of it.

As he threw the ball once more for Bramble, he felt that his mother was going to come to the window and call his name. A second later it happened. He was getting good at sensing things, he decided. He could even hear his father coming downstairs, although he should have been too far away from the house to hear his footsteps. He also knew that something was being said about his father going away on a trip again. Bramble could sense something also; Dill could tell by the way she dropped her ears that there was something not right in the house. He wondered if it was easier to sense things if they were bad.

Slowly they walked towards the back porch. Dill took a quick look at Bramble's paws and reckoned she was clean enough to come into the kitchen with him.

Both his parents were sitting at the table talking.

'I *do* feel things and I can't believe you would say that,' his father was saying.

'What, and *I* don't?'

The atmosphere was tense, but as Dill entered the room his father turned and looked at him and tried to smile.

'Son, I've got to go on a trip, but it's not for long and I promise you that you'll love the surprise I bring back for you.'

'It's only for a few days,' his mother added in a chirpy voice that didn't match the moment, 'and wait till you see what he brings back.'

Dill smiled back at her, looking for light to appear around her the way it used to when she was truly happy. It wasn't there.

His father reached over and ruffled his son's blond hair with his big hand.

'Be a good boy and look after your mother while I'm away,' he said, 'and I promise I'll have much more time to play with you when I get back.'

He reached out his other hand in the direction of the dog and invited her to jump up onto his lap, which she did without hesitation. As she began to lick his face, though, he tried to push her away.

'Get off, you big soppy thing,' he laughed.

For the first time in ages Dill saw a faint circle of light around his father's body. But then it was gone.

After supper Dill had to wash and get ready for bed, and Bramble had to be fed and wiped down with a damp towel. She was to be spared the humiliation of a bath that night, which was good, because it meant she would be allowed to be with him in his room again.

Dill climbed the small wooden staircase that led to his bedroom, headed for the big old-fashioned bed and got under the covers.

The room was still full of unopened boxes with stuff from his old house, so there wasn't much room for him to play there yet, but he did like the room, even though the walls were covered with old flowery wallpaper which made it look like his grandma's bedroom and there were no curtains on the windows yet. But that was good too, because he loved this time of night when he could still see for miles in the fading light.

Every night he would see animals and large birds moving around outside, and he especially loved to watch a family of rabbits who would come into the garden beneath his window. They would bounce around and then stop and drop their ears down onto their backs, and it made him laugh when their noses moved up and down. He always thought that they were talking to one another when they did that. Sometimes he even thought he could hear them speaking inside his head. Maybe he could, in the same way that he did with the dog. There was always a special feeling that touched him in this twilight time before sleep. His world felt empty for a moment, empty of all feeling.

Bramble bounced up the stairs and came into the room. She pushed her brown and white nose towards Dill's face and kissed him on the cheek the way she always did, then walked around in circles for a moment the way she always did, before collapsing in a heap on the floor and letting out a loud sigh. Dill sighed with her; it was as if their breathing had synchronised.

He was becoming tired now, and his body and mind relaxed as he looked out of the window towards the little hills that went up and down all the way to the large hill with the crown of trees and the tall tree in the middle, the one that resembled a hand reaching up to hold the sun by day and now the moon by night. He tried to count the trees, but he couldn't have got past six or seven before he'd fallen into a deep sleep.

Bramble leaped onto the bed beside him, dropped like a sack and let out one more loud sigh, as if she knew it was OK for her to sleep now that her best friend was at peace for another night. There was a light around the animal, and it appeared to expand and encompass the boy, as if it was holding him in a protective membrane.

The dog finally followed the boy into peaceful sleep at the same time as the small bedroom window turned black, hiding the rugged world they now lived in.

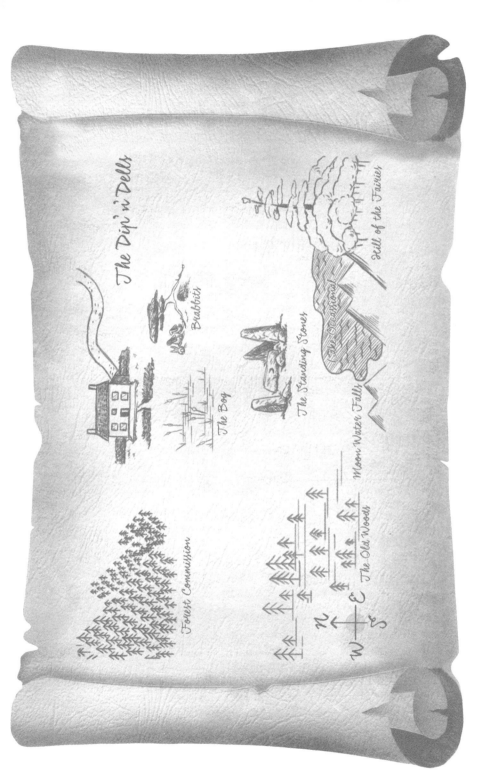

The Dip'n'Dells

Chapter Two
The Dip 'n' Dells

The dip 'n' dells was a very strange place. It was as far north as anyone could go by road. It was almost untouched by humans except for a small burst of dark green pine trees which formed the shape of a triangle on the side of a low, sloping hillside that had been planted by a forestry commission between the last main road and the dirt track that ran to the old white stone cottage. The cottage itself looked completely out of place, as if it had dropped out of the sky and landed on the only flat square of land for miles.

The house was called Moon Cottage and had been built by Dill's great-great-grandparents, who had chosen to move their family as far away from civilisation as they could, as they felt that the world was becoming a very bad place to live in at the time, which was during the Second World War. They had acquired the land simply by staking claim to it, following an old law in that part of the country. No one had ever objected, quite simply because there had never been any interest in the land from developers or farmers because of how incredibly difficult the terrain was.

The nearest village lay almost 20 miles to the south of the cottage and was called Upper Dell. It was made up of a scattering of small dwellings, a village hall, a pub-cum-hotel, a village shop/post office and a train station. But a person had to travel to the nearest small town, Dell of Burgh, to fetch proper supplies and catch any sign of real civilisation, and that really only boasted a supermarket, small high street and a farmers' market every other Wednesday.

The amazing thing about places so remote and untouched is the wildlife that inhabits them. In the dells there was an amazing assortment of animals, birds, wild plants and flowers of every description. Small trees grew there which looked as though they had been twisted and deformed like bonsais by the strong winds that came from the north and lasted for weeks. Each had its own character, with branches so gnarled that no use could be made of them in the human world. Little streams turned and twisted their way through small mounds of earth and rock before arriving at a lake, which appeared to be quite full from winter to mid-spring but shrank to half its size come summer, when much of the water was replaced by reeds and bog. Dill's great great-grandparents had christened this patch of water Lake Occasional because of its disappearance and reappearance each year.

To the south and slightly west of the back of the house was a strange little woodland which rose slightly but whose centre looked as though it had sunk into a great hole.

Over to the south-east of the cottage there was a hill which stood out not only because it was the highest hill in the landscape, but because of the tall trees which formed a perfect circle at the top of it and the one great Scots pine tree that grew in the middle of the circle, reaching high into the sky above the dells.

It was because of this amazing spectacle that Dill's great-great-grandparents had fallen in love with the place and chosen to settle in this remote yet strangely beautiful part of the world. On their honeymoon they had headed as far north as they could go and pitched a small tent in the exact spot where the cottage now stood. They had been amazed that every night the moon appeared to sit for a moment on top of the trees like a huge white pearl on top of a crown, hence the name of their house when they got permission to build it several years later.

'Moon Cottage' had remained in the family and had served as a great retreat, a place in which they could disappear from the world when it became too much for them, as was the case with Dill's family at the present time.

To say that Dill's world had completely changed was no exaggeration; nothing in the dip 'n' dells resembled anything from his life before. His old house had been in a street with lots of houses that all looked the same. He had lived there with his mother and father and sometimes his grandma and sometimes his sister, who had been sick since he was quite young. He only had a few real memories of her sharing his life. One was of when they had played on a beach together, and another was of a Christmas when the house was full of gifts and they had fought to rip open as many as they could, not caring who they belonged to. Happy memories of a happy home.

There had also been lots of children his age to play with. Toby was his best friend – well, they played in each other's gardens and walked to school together. Dill's garden was a small square of short, neatly cut grass with a high brown wooden fence around it that blocked the other gardens from sight, although everybody could hear everybody else's chatter over the fences. His school seemed big and loud, as did the park, which was by his house. It had climbing frames and swings and was always full of people making lots of noise.

One of Dill's favourite things was to go swimming in the swimming baths with Toby and his father on a Saturday morning and then on to the high street, which was filled end to end with shops and pizza places and burger bars and ice-cream places and lots of people walking around all the time. And there was a football field where Bramble loved to go and chase her tennis ball and the sticks people threw for her.

Things had definitely changed since he last went to school with his friends and played in his small garden with Toby. In fact they had begun before, as he had seen less and less of Toby while his sister was ill. Sometimes he'd wondered if Toby's mum and dad could see the darkness around his family and didn't want their son to come and play with him.

Then he'd been sent to his grandmother's house for a bit, and after that there had been the passing of his sister. He'd been brought back to his own house for the funeral or, as he thought of it, 'the Dark Day', when everyone in his house wore black clothes to say goodbye to Amber. Even he'd been given a small black suit and tie to wear, clothes he'd never seen before. He had no idea where they were now. The changes in his parents had appeared more exaggerated to him around this time; they'd become so quiet with him and with each other. After all that, to be plucked out of his not-so-normal life and dropped into a vast wilderness like the dip 'n' dells was quite a lot for a young boy to take in.

It had all happened so quickly. One day, just a couple of weeks after his tenth birthday (which was 17th September), he'd been in his small garden with his dog and been told that his family was moving, and the next thing he was being driven in his father's car to what felt like the very end of the world: a place in the middle of nowhere with just one dirt road, one old stone house and no one else anywhere near it.

The area had a daft name, the dip 'n' dells, and didn't look anything like the countryside his parents and grandparents would take him to. He was used to countryside having square-shaped fields, proper paths and neat lines of trees all the same size. This place was rough, and nothing looked as if it had been planted deliberately. There were no fences either, not even round the house, just a small wall made of different-sized stones covered in greenish moss with big ferns and leaves growing out of it.

There were no high streets or shops or swings in this strange new world, and no Toby to go swimming or play with. It looked as though nothing ever happened there and no one ever wanted to visit it. It was just wild, with lots of bumps sticking out of the ground, strange small trees and in some places large rocks. The unusual crooked nature of the landscape kept it clear of people and projects, which meant that it was as natural and untouched as at the beginning of time.

Like most places on Earth that people don't inhabit, nature had made it her own. One of the things Dill soon started to love about the dells was how many new animals and birds he saw there. Every day brought new birds, some bright yellow with long black tails that wagged up and down, others with little golden crests sticking up from their heads and bright red flashes on their small wings. Some big birds would circle high above him in the sky or hover with wings that flapped hundreds of times but took them nowhere, just kept them suspended in mid-air.

Besides all these there were the animals he could see each night from his window, like the rabbits who looked as though they were having a conversation. One night he saw a deer appearing and disappearing through the dells like shadow. He saw a badger for the first time, and squirrels, which were red, not grey like the ones in the park near his old house. He saw a heron standing on one leg on the boggy ground behind the wall, trying to catch frogs and toads in its long beak. It wasn't long before he felt that there was more to this place than he had first thought.

Learning about the natural world was to be part of the new curriculum his mother had planned for him; she would take on the role of his teacher for the coming year. She had been a schoolteacher before he was born and then again until his older sister got sick. Now she wanted to spend some time helping her son learn and sharing some togetherness with him. She wanted to rebuild a connection to him after all the time she had spent on Amber.

Dill had often been told by his grandma how good a teacher his mother was. She loved to tell her grandson how smart and happy his mother used to be and how proud she was of her only daughter. And it pleased him to listen to his grandma's stories, because they were always about good things and good times. He especially loved to hear her talk about his grandpa who'd gone to heaven, because she didn't seem sad about it. In fact she often said that he was still with her and that he even came to visit her when she was asleep and it made her happy when she woke.

Grandma gave off a different feeling from his parents when she spoke about heaven. Her heaven was bright and happy and genuinely made her light; it wasn't in any way disturbing to Dill. The one thing the boy missed most in the dells was his grandmother. There was so much he wanted to show her in his crazy yet comforting new world.

Grandma had told him that the dip 'n' dells was a very special place and that it was important for his family to go there now because it would help his parents. She'd said that it was 'pure', and he didn't know why, but something in the way she'd said the word made him feel that it was magical. That was the thing about Grandma – she had the same way of knowing that he and Bramble did. His tummy would feel something when she said certain words, and sometimes when she didn't speak he would hear her thoughts, or at least imagine he did.

She often spoke to him about the place she'd grown up in and talked about a special tree there called the wish tree. She said that it was hundreds of years old and that fairies lived in it, and when she was a girl she was taken there by her own grandmother, who showed her how to make wishes come true. She promised that one day she'd take Dill there, but he would have to keep it a secret or the wishes wouldn't come true. The fairies of the dells knew everything and they would know if a person told a secret.

Dill had heard such stories since he could remember and they always seemed so far off and unreal. He sort of felt too old to think about them, but now he was actually here, it felt as though the dip 'n' dells did hold some kind of magic. He wondered if the wish tree was the one on top of the high hill with the crown of trees around it. From his bedroom window he could see that tree standing out above all of the others. Every time he looked at it he felt that something was pulling him towards it and that if he were allowed to go out of the garden, that would be the first place he would head for; that or the little lake, which was on the way to the hill anyway, so he figured at some point he would visit both places.

He knew that Bramble had been there because she always headed out that way and most days came back soaking wet. He knew how much fun she had in water and felt bad that he couldn't watch her splashing about.

For a now, although he couldn't explore as much as he wanted, he had time to think about his new home, because all his mother could manage was three hours a day for his tutorials, which meant he had more playtime than ever before. He put up gladly with the maths and English for the first two hours, though they were a bit of a bore, for the last hour was always spent on nature studies. It was great when they studied the creatures of the dells and up to this point it had been warm enough to do most sessions in the large unkempt garden.

For all his mother seemed to know about the dells, though, he instinctively knew that his grandma knew much more. He wondered if the stories she told him before bed, which always had some kind of magical events in them, were actually true stories of her childhood. They always made him feel good, and he would try to remember them in the quiet of his room when it was difficult to sleep.

His memories of kicking a ball with Toby were already beginning to fade. Different things happened in the dip 'n' dells. Often when playing on his own in the garden Dill would look up at the sky and find his gaze fixed on what looked like shapes in the clouds above him. Sometimes he would be certain he saw people and the next moment he would snap out of it. What was happening to him? What was real and what wasn't? Why didn't he know? Was it the place, or maybe how he was feeling, or both, or was it his imagination taking over because he had no one really to talk to?

He felt sure that when his grandma came he could tell her about it. He could also tell her how he and Bramble seemed to know what each other was thinking, and how his mother and father's voices would speak to him when they were silent, and how he always knew when they were keeping things from him.

He somehow understood that all these things were connected to the strange new world he'd found himself in. He wanted to get out and explore more of it, but he had a feeling that this would only happen when his grandma arrived. He really, really hoped that would be soon.

Chapter Three

The Old Woman Arrives

It was the second last day of October when Dill's mother came into his bedroom early and announced that his father would be home that day and that he had a great surprise for him. She seemed to be much happier than usual and didn't even notice that there was a brown and white fluffy head with long brown curly ears on the pillow.

Bramble had overslept. She knew that she had to get off the bed before Dill's mother was awake and normally she would leap down onto the floor early and curl up in her place, which was at the foot of Dill's bed on an old blanket, but she had been out in the wild countryside for hours the day before and had been really tired.

Now she stretched out beside Dill, forcing him to the edge of the bed, yawned away the sleep from her body, then sprang to her feet and looked down at him. She leaned her soft furry face over his, which made her eyes droop and her long ears hang down over his head, and her soft velvet lips seemed to drop loosely from her mouth as she launched into what Dill called 'spaniel attack'.

Great big fat spaniel kisses were soaking the boy's face as he giggled and tried to fight the dog off, but this was a full-blown onslaught of affection, the type that only happened in the morning when he woke or when he'd come back from somewhere and Bramble wanted to tell him how much she'd missed him.

Dill struggled to sit up, because he wanted to see his dog do the one thing he loved more than anything else: a crinkle. Bramble was the only dog he'd ever seen who would crinkle up her nose and lips then bare her teeth and start laughing like a hyena. Most people got a half-crinkle when they came through the door, but Dill always found that a full-blown crinkle would follow a spaniel attack.

He was laughing so loudly now that it alerted his mother to what was going on.

'Get that crazy dog off your bed, boy!' she called out. But the way she said it told him that neither he nor his dog was in any real trouble today.

In the kitchen, eggs were rattling around in a pan of bubbling water and Dill was aware that his mother was giving off a bubbling sensation as well. He noticed that when Bramble bounded in she greeted his mother with a half-crinkle, something she hadn't done since they'd moved to the dells. This told Dill that something good was happening, and he knew it was when his mother crouched down to the dog and ruffled her ears with both hands and for a fleeting moment she was outlined in white light.

The kitchen was warm, the big open fire burning hot with orange flames, but outside a cold mist was covering the ground, which made it difficult to see the wild bushes and shrubs that made up the garden. Beyond this was a wall of solid grey which kept the dells completely hidden from view. On any other day Dill might have felt shut in, but today it seemed to him that the elements were giving him a warm cosy hug.

After breakfast and two hours of schooling from his mother, he looked up from his arithmetic book and noticed that the mist had lifted and it was bright outside. This was great, because his mother had promised him that if the weather lifted she'd go out with him as part of his nature studies and show him some of the walks she'd done as a child. This would be the first time he'd been allowed to leave the garden since their arrival.

Dressed in their heaviest coats and Wellington boots, Dill and his mother stomped off through the marshy ground immediately behind the garden; Bramble, on the other hand, high-tailed it over the wall like a cannon-ball and disappeared in a flash.

The ground felt squashy under Dill's feet, but he was excited to be venturing out into the landscape he'd only been able to look at for the past three weeks. His mother seemed lively too. She was talkative – in fact the most talkative she'd been since they had arrived.

'Oh, I missed this place, Dill,' she said, relaxing her shoulders and letting her head fall back. 'Did you know that I spent whole summers here with Grandma when I was a girl?'

Dill could see that her energy was growing. He could feel it too.

'What was your favourite place to play in when you came here, Mum?'

'Oh, let me see. Yeah, it has to be the old wood, because it goes down into a kind of gorge and is filled with the most magical carpet of flowers. I got to see so many wonderful species of animals, birds and plants there, which was great, because I was studying science at the time.'

It was clear to Dill that his mother had never seen the dip 'n' dells the way he or his grandma did, but he was happy that she was becoming more animated. As they walked together she pointed out where different birds made their nests in the springtime and where and when was best to watch animals feeding.

There wasn't actually much wildlife on view, yet there seemed to be a special feeling about the day, Dill thought. The light appeared to be different somehow. The sun was hovering directly above the tallest tree, the one on top of the highest hill. It looked huge hanging there in the sky, which was clear except for a few thin clouds gathering in the east.

To their right there was the old wood, which seemed to be sinking into the ground, but today the trees looked full and proud. The colours of the leaves were particularly special – yellow, orange, red and shimmering gold. It was as though every leaf on every tree was showing itself off in one last attempt to be noticed before the winter stripped it of its beauty. The light wind made them all tremble in such a way that they seemed to be applauding themselves for a fine display.

Dill and his mother had reached some rocks which looked as though they had broken away from the main group in the dells and formed a circle on their own. As they climbed up one of the smaller ones, Dill realised they were bigger than he had first thought. His view of the dip 'n' dells was much wider from this point and he now knew why there wasn't much wildlife on display: Bramble was running to the left and then crossing back to the right, the way she'd done in the park in the old place, quartering the ground till she'd covered every inch, looking for things to flush out and chase.

Dill's mother gave a whistle and the dog stopped in her tracks, a bit bewildered at first, as she'd been allowed to run out on her own since coming to the dells. She looked back at Dill and his mother, lifted her right front paw and tilted her head to the left as if waiting for the next command.

'Bramble, come here!' Dill's mother called in strong voice, making a gesture with her right hand.

Immediately the dog started to run towards them.

Dill saw that his mother's face was red with the cold, but it made her look much more alive than she had for some time. A light was back in her eyes, and even though she'd got thinner recently, Dill thought that she looked strong.

She noticed him staring at her and smiled at him. A faint light was starting to build around her head again and it got brighter as she held her smile.

'This is where Grandma comes to think, you know.'

She looked around the circle of stones, crinkling up her nose like the dog's half-crinkle and frowning at the same time.

'It never did it for me, but she swears by it, says things come to her when she sits here. She can be strange at times, your old grandma!'

Her face relaxed back to a smile once more and then she and Dill both burst out laughing as Bramble stood up on her hind legs, staggered sideways and barked at them. Dill was certain that he heard her say, 'Oi! Can I go off now?' He looked at his mother, but she didn't seem to have heard.

He had a sudden urge to tell her about the strange things that had been happening to him lately, but then he stopped himself. An inner knowing told him that he should just keep her happy and smiling and surrounded with the light that told him she was OK.

Over her left shoulder he could see the high hill with the crown of trees. The clouds were starting to get much thicker above them and as they began to mask the sunlight, something was beginning to form in them. At first it wasn't clear, then Dill realised it was a woman. He had seen her earlier that week, he recalled, but today he could make out much more of what she looked like.

His mother moved on to a separate stone and started looking the other way, over her right shoulder, twisting her neck back towards Moon Cottage as though she was being magnetically pulled in that direction. Dill, however, was compelled to focus his attention on the woman in the clouds.

She was middle-aged, he thought, older than his mother, yet not as old as his grandma. She had dark red hair flowing behind her and her clothes were the colour of the leaves on the trees in the old wood. Her hands were outstretched in front of her, as if she had taken something from the ground below her, and she appeared to be moving away from the Earth and wrestling with the clouds, which were pulling her higher into the sky.

Dill's mind said that the whole scene was an effect of the clouds, but the inner knowing that had stopped him speaking to his mother earlier compelled him to stand and watch.

Time stood still and everything other than the lady seemed to recede from Dill. His head was clear, yet swirling like the clouds above him. Images moved quickly through his mind like a film reel, too quickly for him to catch anything clearly, but he seemed to feel the word 'change' inside his head. Change, change, change… 'It's time for change,' said a woman's voice in his mind.

'Bramble! Come out of there!'

His mother's voice snapped Dill out of it and brought him back to the stones on which they were perched. He turned his head to see that the dog was black with mud from the bog.

'Honestly, that dog! Let's head back and clean her up,' his mother said in an exasperated tone.

Surprised, Dill stared at her. The light around her had faded. She turned quickly away from him, jumped down from the stone and headed back in the direction of the cottage.

Dill could hear silent sobs coming from her and somehow he knew this wasn't to do with Bramble at all, but to do with his sister and the cottage. Something had happened to drag her back into her grief.

He jumped to the ground as well, and as he landed, he came back down to Earth. A different reality filled his thoughts as he plodded back to the house.

In the small back porch Bramble was sitting in an old tin bath having water poured over her from a red plastic watering-can. Her body looked much thinner than when she was dry and fluffy; in fact she looked a bit scrawny as she trembled under the jet of water.

Dill felt sad, not only for the dog who was shaking in the bath, but for his mother, who was silently carrying out Bramble's cleansing. The dog loved water and took every opportunity to splash around in puddles or ponds, but being bathed by his parents was a penance she had to endure.

As he squeezed passed his mother, she was mumbling to herself, 'Dog, filthy,' and 'Grounded, I mean it.'

She stopped and looked up at her son and realised that his mood had changed just as hers had.

Giving him one of her best fake smiles, she carried on, 'Sometimes she is just so much work – work I really don't need today, Dill. Honestly, I mean... Come on, Bramble, out of there. Go into the garden now.'

Too late – Bramble was shaking her soaking wet fur so furiously that the water was spraying all over Dill's mother and the porch.

Dill's eyes widened, as he thought she would shout at the dog, but to his surprise she let out a loud burst of hysterical laughter and bent her body forward, clasping both her hands to her very wet chest. She looked up at him again and he realised that even though she was drenched, she was smiling properly again.

'Oh, Dillan, I'm so sorry that I got cross,' she said, 'but I'd cleaned this house today because of the news I got from your father and I didn't want anything to spoil it.'

Dill knew that wasn't the real reason why her mood had changed at the stones, but he said nothing. He was becoming used to good moments followed by bad ones.

'Your father called very early this morning,' his mother continued, 'and told me that he was bringing your grandma to stay with us. Isn't that great news?'

She was still sort of laughing and shaking as she spoke, and was trying hard to put something to the back of her mind. She could do this by revealing the secret.

And it *was* great news. It was the best thing that had happened since he'd been in the cottage, thought Dill. He suddenly remembered that he'd dreamed that morning that he was greeting his grandma on the dirt path in front of the house. In the dream she was wearing a long black coat with a red scarf around her neck, and she'd brought books for him, although he'd never got to see them because they were in a large black suitcase.

'That's great news, Mum. Did you hear that, Brams? Grandma's coming!'

The dog's wet ears lifted and she turned her head slightly in acknowledgement.

Dill's mother dried the dog with one of the old towels that were kept for just that purpose, then made her sit by the fire. Dill joined her and put his arms around her neck.

As his mother watched the scene, some of the good feelings of the morning started to come back to her. She took a deep breath and shook her head to ward off the tears that were building in her eyes; she was determined to be strong for her son that day.

Dill had drifted into a half-nap when he felt the dog's body jerk; her head shot up at the same time, her now bone-dry ears fluffed out to their fullest. This could only mean one thing: someone was approaching the house, and he knew exactly who that someone was.

Before he could get to his feet, Bramble shot off, leaving him so unbalanced that he almost fell flat on his face. He scrambled to his feet and raced after her. He found her at the end of the dim hallway that led to the front door, scratching at the dark wooden door and making high-pitched yelps.

Dill could hear his mother running downstairs as he turned the brass knob and yanked the stiff old door backwards. There was a kerfuffle in the doorway as he and Bramble fought to get out first. The dog won.

As Dill emerged, he could see his father opening the passenger door of his car and his grandma trying to get out. The whole thing looked very strained, as she had the big spaniel's front paws on her lap, pushing her back into the car.

'Get down, Bramble,' he heard his father say.

As he approached the car, his grandma was looking a bit shaken, but she said, with a big genuine smile across her face, 'Full-blown spaniel attack, I think, Dill?'

Her black coat was covered in white hair from the dog as she wrapped her arms around her grandson. He was so happy, yet tears were running down his face before he knew it. They were his grandma's. His mother and father were hugging too, and Bramble was leaping off all four legs like a spring lamb, which led everyone to stop and wait for what was coming next.

'Crinkles!' everybody shouted, as the spaniel did her best and most impressive trick, bringing great laughter to the scene.

Grandma had two cases brought in from the car, one small and brown and the other large and black. She told Dill that she had brought him presents.

'I bet you can't guess what,' she said, smiling.

Instantly his reply shot out of his mouth: 'Books, Grandma! You brought me books.'

There was silence for a second as both his parents looked bewildered, but Grandma simply raised her left eyebrow in a knowing kind of way and said, 'Of course I did,' as she hung her coat on a hook by the front door. 'I'm starving,' she added loudly, and headed for the kitchen, following the smell that was emanating from the big oven.

The dinner they ate that night was the best dinner ever. It was even better, Dill thought, than Christmas dinner or his favourite of all, pizza. There was something so comforting in sitting listening to grown-up conversation when it was upbeat. There was excitement in the air that night and even without examining the words that were spoken, he knew things were good.

'I've sorted almost everything my end, Tom, save for a few last-minute things, and am now free to be here as long as you need me,' Grandma was saying. Her words sounded bouncy and uplifting.

'Thanks. I've sorted out my work too,' his father replied, 'so everything's starting to come together.'

'I hope you've all left room for some of this delicious apple pie and ice cream,' his mother cut in.

Dill felt as though he was floating on air. For a moment he had to hold back from actually crying.

Finally the big wooden table was empty of plates and dishes, but for a while they stayed there anyway. Dill's grandma was telling his parents all sorts of things that made them smile, and there was a light in the cottage that hadn't been there before. And it wasn't coming from the bulb in the ceiling or the glow of the fire, but from the people sitting round the table.

It was a surprise when Dill heard his father say that they should all go into the living room, because he had forgotten that they had one. The only time he'd seen it, it had been full of boxes and he'd only been able to open the big wooden door halfway. He was quite amazed to see that there were no boxes in there now and that it had furniture and an even bigger fireplace than the kitchen, with a great big fire already alight. The sofas and the big rug on the wooden floor had come from his old house, and he loved how comfortable it all was. He sank into a sofa beside his grandma, who carefully placed her cup of tea on a small wooden table he hadn't seen before, then took the long red scarf from around her neck, spread it over his shoulders and pulled him close to her body.

'I'm glad I got here now, because come the wintertime, my God, you will see snow up here. Ha, ha, ha, you've never seen snow like dells snow.'

His grandma's laughter sounded so friendly, Dill thought as he snuggled into her side, trying to catch every word she said. He didn't know if it was the heat from the fire or his grandma's soothing voice, but he was finding it difficult to keep his eyes open. Normally it took him ages to go to sleep in Moon Cottage and it was only when he felt Bramble beside him that he drifted into slumber. But now he heard the loudest noise a child will experience, which is the deafening thud of heavy eyelids that have been beaten down by sleep.

Dill woke in his bedroom with no memory of going there; in fact his father had carried him up to bed the previous night. He sat up and looked around for Bramble, but she wasn't there. It was strange for him not to have his best friend there when he woke up, so he jumped out of bed and headed downstairs to the kitchen, only to find that it was empty and quiet apart from the logs crackling on the fire.

'How strange,' he said out loud. Where was his mother? She was always in the kitchen when he came downstairs.

He went to the back porch, where the door stood open, and called for Bramble, but nothing happened. She was nowhere in sight and he had no sense of her presence.

Back up in his bedroom, he was dressing when he heard people going into the kitchen. He recognised his parents' voices, so dashed down to join them.

'Where's Grandma and where's Bramble?' he squawked excitedly, looking from one to the other.

'Oh, they went out ages ago,' his father told him calmly. He was holding a large paper sack with something round inside.

There was a sense of normality about the moment, Dill realised. It had no darkness, no strangeness – which did actually make it strange somehow. He rubbed his eyes with the backs of his hands and tried to understand what was going on.

'Why don't you go out and see if you can find them?' his mother suggested. 'Try the rocks, Dillan, you know that's one of your grandma's special places?'

This was a surprise. Dill hadn't been allowed to leave the garden on his own before; in fact, it was only yesterday that he'd been allowed to leave it at all. Quick as a flash, he was forcing his feet into his wellies, then scarpering over the wall and heading out over the marsh towards the low hill at the edge of the old wood.

When he got to the rocks, he climbed onto one and scoured the landscape for his grandma and the dog. It was very cold and he realised he should have worn his warm coat; in fact he was thinking about going back to the house to fetch it when he heard a high-pitched yelping in the distance. It was Bramble, just a distant dot for now, but he could tell that she was heading in his direction.

Standing there looking at the dog, he had the feeling that he was missing something. He looked over to where he'd seen a woman in the clouds the day before. To his amazement, she was still there.

It was hard to pick her out at first, as the sky was full of clouds, but he got glimpses of her dark red hair swinging around and the clouds were full of the colours of her clothes. The yellows and oranges were swirling and spinning, mixing with the shimmery golden light and making the sky look as though it was filled with a fire that was dying down. There almost seemed to be some kind of struggle going on and the air was thick and sticky.

Then, as Dill watched, mesmerised, a great white cloud moved in from the north. It seemed to calm the whole scene and just for a moment the woman's form became clear. She was slowly sinking backwards, as if she'd given up the struggle, and seemed to be fading into the giant white cloud, which had almost come to a stop behind her.

Out of the white cloud, another woman appeared, an older woman with long white hair in a braid which ran all the way down her back. She was much clearer than the other woman and it looked as though she was lowering her right foot from the cloud ready to step down onto the ground.

Only now could Dill see how tall the women were; they appeared to be taller than the trees on the high hill. He was baffled and excited at the same time.

The skin on the older woman's face and hands was such a brilliant white that it had a tinge of blue to it. She was in a white nightgown which came all the way down to her ankles and she was holding a pole or a staff in her hand and seemed to be placing it on the ground close to her blue-white foot.

So caught up was Dill in this vision that he was only aware of his grandma and Bramble arriving when he heard a clatter on the rock he was standing on. It was his grandma's stick; she always carried it with her, even though she could walk perfectly well, and now she was tapping it against the rock to get his attention. His connection to the scene in the sky was broken so suddenly that he felt as though he'd been shot through by lightning.

'What can you see, boy?' his grandma was shouting. 'Tell me what you can see in the sky, Dill!'

Dill didn't reply. He didn't know how to. It would sound so stupid.

He scrambled off the rock and stood before his grandma. She took his arm and this time she spoke to him in a whisper.

'Dill, what did you see? Tell me what you were watching – I promise you, it won't sound stupid.'

Without thinking, he began to reel off, 'There was a woman in the sky, a huge woman who was old but not that old, and her hair was dark red...'

He was completely out of breath by the time he'd finished the whole story. He wasn't sure what to expect back, but what did come was a shock.

Looking skywards, his grandma whispered, 'So, she's here then. The old woman has arrived.'

33

Chapter Four
The Goddesses

Grandma was sitting on a boulder covered in green spongy moss at the foot of the large rocks, her hand covering her mouth as she pondered on what had just happened. She knew exactly what was going on and who the women were, but she had never thought that her grandson would be able to experience such phenomena. She had always thought it would be his sister.

A memory of her own grandmother flashed into her mind. Grams was a magical person who had a real love of the dells. She would gently impart her wisdom at the very moment her granddaughter was ready to grasp it. It was Grams who had introduced her to the powers of nature and to a new language of feeling. She had given her a healthy understanding of life, and of death, which had wiped away her fears and steered her safely through her life so far.

Her mind shifted for a second to the last time she had seen her grandmother. It was in what was now Dill's bedroom in Moon Cottage. She remembered holding the old lady's hand.

'I'm ready to leave now,' Grams had said quietly. 'The lady in the sky is waiting for me. I always knew it would be the old one; she told me once when I was young, but I never paid much attention to her then.'

There was a pause and both ladies turned to look out of the window at a large white moon cutting through billowing white clouds.

Grandma breathed in and was back in that moment on this very day so many years before. It was on 31st October that her own grandmother had left this world, on the day the goddesses had changed over.

Dill was captivated as he stood watching his grandma sitting there in silence. She looked different somehow. Maybe it was because she was wearing a funny green hat with small brown feathers in it that he'd never seen before and a dark green cape over her coat. But then he realised that it wasn't what she was wearing that made her seem different, it was what he was feeling in his gut. He was sensing a change in her, a change that made her look much younger and feel different somehow, almost as if she was a different person. For a second he had the feeling that if he wanted, he could peer through the window of her memories, but he knew not to, so he spoke instead.

'Grandma, what did you mean when you said she was here?'

She looked up at him and slowly began to nod her head. 'Yes, I should talk to you about this place, I suppose.' In an almost silent whisper, she added, 'After all, I did wish this for you.'

She quickly motioned for him to sit on the comfy moss-covered stone beside her.

Dill settled down and looked at her expectantly, his big blue eyes wide open.

Half-turning her body to face him, she said, 'OK, let me start with the ladies.'

And she took off her cloak and wrapped it around his shoulders, which were shaking with cold.

'When I was a child of half your age I saw them. There are more than two of them; there are actually four. The four ladies of change live somewhere between the land and the sky. They are the goddesses of the seasons and they look after all the elements that exist in their space and their time. Not everyone can see them and I never imagined that you would. That's why I never told you about them before, not even in the stories I told you.'

The boy's brows were deeply furrowed as he took in every syllable.

'Not everyone can see them,' his grandmother went on, 'or connect with this place. Your mother never did. She loved it at times, but she was never a part of it. And I always just assumed that it would be Amber who would share what my grandmother shared with me – this knowing, this understanding.'

She seemed to be struggling with her choice of words, almost addressing herself at times, being careful to say the right thing to her grandson. Dill began to feel what she was saying rather than hear it. He stopped trying to listen and just absorbed the sound of the words.

'It's all to do with this place. It is a very special place. There are other special places too, but this place is powerful. The seasons here are different from the normal seasons, Dill. Yes, there are four of them and they are winter, spring, summer and autumn, but they aren't measured by a calendar or by an actual date, but by the ladies you saw. When they change over, the season changes. When the new lady arrives, the season is hers, no matter what day it is.'

She went on to explain that all the creatures of the dells could sense when a goddess's time was coming to a close, as there were signs that the new one was on her way.

'You saw one and the other was behind her. That's a sign that change is coming. Nothing just happens, Dill, they always warn us.'

She said that each goddess stayed for around three months, but if the season had to be extended or shortened, it would be so. There was no point in counting days.

'In the time of each goddess, life is different. The things that happen are different, just as the weather and landscape are different and what you think you know is different. Each of the ladies teaches us a lesson, and it will be something that is relevant to our life if we take note of it, Dill.'

She stopped talking, looked up at the sky and smiled in a knowing way. Then she took another breath, a much slower one, as if she was preparing to do something. She gently closed her eyes and continued, only now she let her heart talk to her grandson rather than her voice. Dill also closed his eyes and absorbed what the old lady was giving him.

'The first lady you saw, the one with the long dark red hair and colourful clothes, she is called Ercesha, and she is the goddess of autumn. When she first appears, it is to let all the creatures in the dells know that the good times and abundance of summer are about to end and to remind them that they should begin to think about storing food, because she brings change. Birds who come here in the summer know the moment she arrives and they start to eat more to build up strength for the long flight they must make to find the summer goddess, whom they follow. The little red squirrels, they know that when the autumn goddess is here they must store supplies for the coming winter. Ercesha makes us aware that there will always be changes in our lives and that we must never ignore them, but act on them if we have the chance to. She is a wise woman.'

Dill thought about how his father was storing up logs in the old shed at the back of the cottage and how his mother had made a journey to town recently and brought back tons of food for the freezer. He felt that he understood what his grandmother was saying.

It was amazing that she'd seen the same things as he had when she was half his age. How strange, he thought. He wanted to ask her about it, but thought better of it. She was carrying on talking about the sky women and he felt compelled to listen.

Grandma was explaining that Cailasha was the name of the old lady with the long white braid.

'The reason you saw her stepping down towards the ground is that it is her time to take over as guardian of the sky. When she actually touches the ground with her foot, the frost will come and autumn will be over. She will bang her staff on the ground and snow will cover the dells in a way you've never seen. She will hold the Earth prisoner until her strength is gone and her time is over and the new goddess takes over.'

Dill half-opened his eyes and gazed at his grandmother as she spoke. The way she was explaining things was bringing the entire scene to life in his mind, but, he suddenly realised, her lips weren't moving at all. This was so baffling, but strangely natural – it was the way he'd been able to hear voices coming from his parents and the dog, only this time his grandma was actually *making* it happen.

She nodded her head and he instinctively knew that he was correct in what he was thinking. Another nod told him that she wanted him to close his eyes and pay attention as she let the rest of the story unfold.

'My own grandmother taught me the names of the goddesses. She had such a connection to this land. She said that each lady had the power to change circumstances and that if you were in the right place at the right time when the goddess was in her full power, then she could change your destiny – remove you from one path and put you on another.'

It was the spring goddess that Grandma loved more than any other because she was so vibrant and full of life.

'Her name is Brigisha and she is the young one – childlike in appearance, but, boy, is she strong.'

She let out a short burst of laughter, which caused Dill to do the same.

'She looks wild and unkempt, like this land, and has bushy strawberry-blonde hair with flowers and leaves knotted through it.'

Another little laugh.

'She wears bedraggled yellow clothes with dirt stains over them because of the way she arrives, which is by bursting through the cold, hard Earth with a bang and a show of youthful vibrancy, throwing Cailasha back into the sky.'

More laughter followed and Dill could feel his grandma's body bobbing up and down.

She also loved Brigisha because she brought warmth and light back to the dells and reminded everything that life could renew itself.

'When you see the amazing colours of the wild flowers that spring up through the ground behind her and all the birds and animals coming out to celebrate her arrival, it's truly magical.'

The feeling in Dill when Grandma was describing the spring goddess was intense. It was as if he was filling up with air or light or something he didn't know, but it felt magical, especially when she said out loud, 'She gives all of us the strength to go on, son.'

Then there was a long pause as the old lady drew another deep breath into her body and once again closed her eyes. Dill was thinking, 'Summer, what about the summer woman?' when she gave a little knowing giggle at her grandson's instant grasp of this inner language and flowed back into the story.

'It is the summer goddess, Lassaisha, who never has to struggle to take over. She simply walks in slowly when she knows that Brigisha's energy has expired. She is a woman in the fullness of life who appears taller than the others. She is very slender, with silky golden red hair all the way down to her waist. She is generous and her season is stable and calm; she nurtures and heals through her warmth and brightness. She is the keeper of summertime and many creatures follow her wherever she goes. Her time is a time of contentment and tranquillity. She is special because she holds up the beauty of the Earth for all to see. Many pains are healed in her time, many wrongs corrected.'

She went on to tell Dill about all the seasonal changes and how important it was for the inhabitants of the dip 'n' dells to understand them.

'Each new season brings different elements, which means that all life-forms have to learn to adapt. Those who don't will perish, but not because nature is cruel – no, nature moves in one direction, that's all, and those who push against it will be trampled by her mighty force. We must all move with her, Dill.'

He instantly understood her words, as they seemed to be accompanied by pictures of animals, birds and plants coming to life and dying and coming to life again.

'The goddesses are like daughters of Mother Nature, and the reason they are in places like this is to direct life and teach all the creatures the way of nature and to warn them when change is in the air. Only in the heart of nature are things like life and death truly understood, Dill.'

She said these final words out loud before pushing herself up from the boulder.

'That's enough for today, young man,' she added, as she straightened up by pressing down heavily on her cane, making a noise that sounded like *oowf*. 'There will be many more times when we can come out to the stones and speak sense.'

Dill didn't understand what she meant by speaking sense, but he got to his feet and followed her as she bumbled quickly along the uneven footpath back to the garden. He had so many questions that he wanted to ask her and so much more stuff to tell her about himself, but no sooner had he had the thought than he heard her say, 'Later.' He knew that the words hadn't come from her mouth when she turned her head, still walking forwards, and mumbled, 'Sorry, Dill, hadn't switched off then, tee-hee.'

Dill was shaking his head, not knowing what to think, when out of nowhere something happened that was completely bonkers. Bramble whizzed past Grandma, turned her head towards the old lady and shouted, 'No, you hadn't, dear!' Then she kept on running towards the cottage, giggling loudly, and was out of sight with one leap over the garden wall.

With all that was going on, Dill had completely forgotten that today was Halloween, but when he saw the great big pumpkin lanterns that were in the kitchen window, his mind was pulled away from all of the stuff with Grandma and into the present.

'Look, Dill!' his mother shouted, as she showed off two more pumpkins. 'I saved these for you.'

Dill suddenly realised that the pumpkins must have been what was in the sack his father was holding earlier on.

'Aren't the lanterns lovely, Dill?' Grandma said loudly.

Dill nodded, but was all of a sudden reminded of the speaking thing that had gone on at the rocks.

'Grandma, can I ask you something?'

'Later, when we've all had the lovely lunch your mother's prepared.'

Dill's mother had made a huge plate of sandwiches and even baked cakes earlier that morning. As Dill realised that the table was full of food, it hit him that he hadn't eaten any breakfast and that his stomach was churning with hunger. The rumbling noises coming from it revealed this to everyone in the room as well. Even Bramble looked at him in a very aloof manner that all but said, 'Excuse *you!*'

She was sitting at his grandmother's feet, looking up at her with a pleading expression on her face, trying to persuade her to part with some of the sandwich she was eating. Of course the old lady looked as though she had no idea the dog was there, even when Bramble rested her face on her lap and rolled her big eyes up at her in a way that said, 'Please throw me a crumb, I haven't eaten in weeks.'

As Dill sat down at the table, he thought back to Halloween in the old house. That had been a fun time for him because he had been able to dress up in a costume his mother had made for him. At school there was usually a party and a competition for the best costume. Two years ago he had come second in his pirate's outfit, but Marne Slyfield had come first in her witch's outfit. For a fleeting second he longed to be back there. He also remembered trick or treating, when his mother would walk him around the neighbours' houses in his costume and he'd be given all sorts of goodies like sweets and fruit. Some people had even given him money if they'd run out of other things. Such joyful memories…

Last year he'd missed out on it, though, because his sister had been so sick that he'd had to stay with his grandma, which had meant that he'd missed school too. A heaviness began to pull at his stomach as he thought of that, but it lifted as he recalled that he'd spent that evening with his grandmother and she'd ordered pizza and told him all sorts of stories about the magic of Halloween, which she'd said was the most important day of the year. He couldn't actually remember why, as he'd fallen asleep in the middle of that story. Now he wished he hadn't.

The large wooden table was clear of food now and Dill was scooping mush from one of the large pumpkins his mother had left for him to make a lantern with. Bramble was curled up by the fire, making noises in her sleep. Dill loved it when she did this, as he could imagine what she was dreaming of based on the type of sounds she made. In this one he figured that she was chasing something in the dells, because she was making little high-pitched noises and her body was popping in small involuntary spasms. Dill reckoned that she couldn't catch whatever was in front of her because her soft floppy lips were puffing out with a soft frustrated 'woof-woof' sound.

His parents had gone off in the car to get even more provisions from the nearest town. This meant that they would be gone for quite some time. Dill was thinking that they'd seemed much lighter over lunch when his grandma came over to him and sat in the chair opposite. She reached over the table, took his hand and said that it was time to talk.

She told him that she knew he had lots of questions, but she wanted to know how he was feeling about his new home.

Dill thought for a moment and then said, 'Well, I'm getting used to it and I do love being out in the country with all the wildlife. The birds are amazing, and the animals – wow.'

He stopped and did a little rethink and the old lady waited patiently for him to carry on.

'I suppose being here makes me not think so much about Amber and … you know.'

His big eyes looked right at her. They were like two clear glass windows, behind which was a world of confusion and hurt, but nothing secret or hidden.

Instinctively he spoke about his parents. 'Sometimes they seem so sad, or scared, or angry. I don't like the angry feeling because it isn't loud, like shouting, it's colder and darker and it makes me angry inside.'

He told her how they would have good moments and then bad moments until everything went quiet in the house, only it wasn't really quiet, because that's when other things would happen, like voices that weren't really there.

'How come I could hear what you were saying when you weren't speaking?' he asked.

He also wanted to know about Bramble and how he could have heard her speak in a human voice on two occasions now. It was similar to the unspoken knowing he felt whenever his parents pretended they were happy when they weren't. But he couldn't explain this, and all of the questions just rolled into one long sentence in his mind and he let out a deep sigh of exasperation.

The old lady softened. She had understood everything that he hadn't been able to say. She told him that she would try to explain what he was feeling when he heard things from his parents.

'Because they were feeling so sad after losing Amber, even when they tried to be happy and normal, they just couldn't get back to ordinary life again,' she said. 'There were still so many things to face first. Your sister was sick for a long time, and both your mother and father gave a lot of their time to be with her, and that takes a lot out of a person.'

Dill nodded. He knew this somehow, and when his grandmother said 'time', he got an impression of light.

She tried to make him see that his parents didn't want him to feel their pain but they didn't know that everything they did when he was there would in some way have an effect on him.

'They truly don't know it now, but in time they will understand it,' she said.

And yet again in the boy's mind the word 'time' was replaced by light.

Grandma went on to explain that she hadn't come to Moon Cottage just for a visit but to live with them, as she wanted to help them get through the pain of losing Amber.

'You must understand, Dill,' she said, 'that whenever you need answers, I will be there for you until your parents are ready to talk to you themselves.'

He really did get that, but his mind was also thinking of the other stuff that was going on, the crazy stuff.

Grandma just gave a sort of gentle laugh as he thought that, and said that she would explain to him the language of the dells. She asked him if he remembered that she'd said that they would talk sense again.

'Of course,' he said. It had made no sense at all!

'Sense,' she said, 'is the common language of all the creatures of the dip 'n' dells, and in fact of all people when they are very young. Most people lose their ability to use it because of the modern world around them, with all its distractions and of course human logic – that's what really kills sense in most adult humans.' She shook her head before continuing, 'Sense is a language of inner knowing and it's in everyone or thing that lives, but most people don't use it because they have forgotten how. It is old, very old – like me, Dill.'

Again she laughed.

She told Dill that sense was a form of communication that was natural and instinctive and that you felt it deep inside your stomach, the way he did when he knew his parents were afraid to tell him the truth about how they were feeling.

'Sense is a way of knowing what is truly happening in life,' she said, 'and those who understand it can never be lied to because human words have no bearing on it. That's because it deals with how we truly feel, as it comes from the heart, unlike the words that people speak, which often alter what is true in order to sound right.'

She explained that children who had had a major incident in their lives, like his sister's passing, could experience an increase in their powers of sense because they were forced to go into their inner world, where they would feel more than they listened.

Dill immediately understood. So many times his parents had told him they were OK but he'd felt the pain coming from inside them. When his sister was very ill and just one of his parents had come back from the hospital and taken him places to make up for being away for so long, saying it was to cheer him up, really he had known that they needed cheering up more than him.

Grandma told him that she'd learned to understand sense when she was only about four or five because she'd lived in the dells with her grandparents most of the time while her own parents were away working in the big city where Dill had lived. She said that she'd spent so much of her childhood without using words that her inner voice and instinct had become very strong, and she pointed out to him that he'd developed the ability to sense too, because of the times he'd spent on his own, away from his parents, and the lack of verbal communication in his young life.

Dill suddenly realised that most of the conversations that he had were with himself, inside his head, or with his dog, which again was a silent language of understanding. But he couldn't understand why, if he and his grandma had this ability to communicate without words, this was the first time they'd used it. Why had she waited till now to explain it to him?

Instinctively, the old lady knew how to continue. 'It is this place, Dill, it somehow increases and animates the power of sense, and even though I've been able to use it ever since I can remember, it's only in the dells or places like it where it becomes much clearer, and this is why I never discussed it with you before. There are other reasons too, but now is not the right time for them. Instead, tell me some of the things you've experienced and I'll try to help you understand what was happening.'

Dill started by telling her how strange it had been to hear Bramble speak when she'd whizzed past them earlier that day.

It began to make more sense to him when she explained, 'The dog never actually used words to speak to you, or to me, when she ran past earlier today. She gave off a natural feeling which your human mind translated into words. If she could have turned her feelings into words, what you heard was exactly what she would have said. So you see, you do have the ability to transform feelings into words, and when you truly understand this it will seem perfectly natural. Bramble has always understood your feelings, only now, with the magic of the dells, she can tell you.'

'How brilliant,' Dill thought, and he tried to think things to the dog, who was now awake and looking in his direction. 'Get up and come to me, girl!' he thought. But she never moved, just lay there by the big open fire.

He tried again by thinking that he would get her a treat from her treat jar in the kitchen, but again, nothing. He frowned quizzically at his grandma and she smiled and asked him what he was trying to do.

When she heard, she laughed out loud and said, 'Dillan, it doesn't work too well in the house at the moment. I'll tell you more about that as we go on. And you are *thinking* things to the dog. That's not how it works, son – you have to *feel* something and use that feeling to communicate. Now that will do for tonight. You must finish your lantern before your parents get back and then we'll watch for Cailasha making her appearance over the wish tree and presenting herself to the land. It's quite a spectacle.'

Later that evening grandmother and grandson stood on the flat section of the garden wall to the back and left of the kitchen, both wrapped in thick woollen blankets and looking towards the highest hill in the landscape. The moon was full and so bright that the hill stood out clearly against the night sky. The big spaniel was standing beside them in an elegant pose with her front paws on the wall and back legs stretched out onto the ground, her ears blowing back from her face as the cold wind picked up.

The scene before them became animated as the trees on the hill began to turn white with the first hint of frost from the breath of Cailasha in the sky above them. They could see her form in the light mist that was gathering in the air above the dells. Hypnotised by the shadowy white figure in the brilliant light of the moon, it took them a moment to realise that frost had covered the ground at the very moment that Cailasha had untied the thick knot at the bottom of her long white braid and let her hair free to blow in the wind – a signal of her arrival.

Between the brightness of the moonlight and its reflection on the sparkling ground, night was transformed into day, but not a normal day. It was a strange moment where time wasn't recognised. It didn't exist, not in this place. For a moment this was a thin place, a place where two worlds could become one.

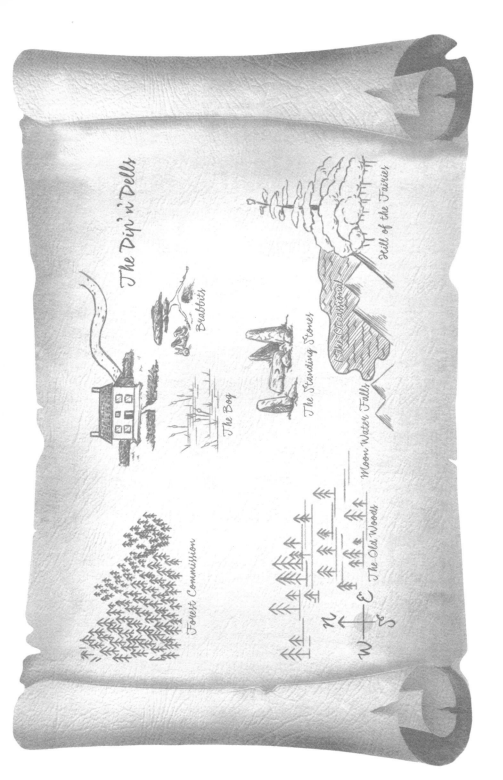

Chapter Five

The Brabbits

The winter goddess had covered the Earth with a blanket of frost to allow Mother Earth time to rest and recuperate after all that she had given of herself over the last three seasons. The creatures who inhabited the dells had known this change was coming. Some had gathered their supplies for winter while others had made warm cosy places to protect themselves from the cold conditions they knew were on the way, but on that particular night the cold white ground didn't seem to matter, as many of the dells creatures were moving over the lumpy, bumpy ground and they were all heading in the same direction: towards the highest hill in the dells.

That hill was known as the hill of the fairies. It stood out from the rest of the landscape not just because of its height but because of the way the trees at the top had grown in an almost perfect circle around the outer rim, forming what looked like a great crown. There was something very special about this place, especially about the magnificent Scots pine that stood at the very centre of the circle. It stood much taller than the other trees and from a distance it looked like a hand reaching up to touch the sky with the tips of its fingers. It was known as the wish tree.

Lots of families in the animal kingdom were on their way to the wish tree that night. One family rushing to get there was the small family of brown rabbits that Dill had often seen from his window. The other dells creatures knew them as the Brabbits. Mrs Brabbit had three small Brabbits bouncing along behind her as she zigzagged her way over the uneven ground, dropping out of sight in the dips and bouncing back up over the dells. This was a very special night for her family and she didn't want to miss it. Her three Brabbit children were doing their best to keep up with her, but she was a seasoned dells runner. She had run and bounced over this landscape all her life and knew every inch of it.

'Come on, kids, keep up a steady rhythm and stay close to Mummy,' she called out to her bunnies. 'And remember, tonight we are quite safe from predators.'

This was true, because it was one of the nights when all of the dells creatures had to refrain from attacking others. There were three other such nights, but tonight was the most important one for the creatures of this land, as it was on this night that the real magic of the place came to life and dreams and wishes could come true.

'This way,' Mrs Brabbit called out to her little brood as she dived head first into a hole at the foot of the hill of the fairies and re-emerged 30 seconds later from a crack at the bottom of a tree halfway up the hill. Her bunnies came flying out after her and kept up the pace she was setting just ahead of them; they were fuelled by excitement tonight.

As the family reached the top of the hill they could see that the gathering was about to begin. Animals of every type had packed themselves into the space around the wish tree and birds of all colours and sizes had filled the branches of the surrounding trees.

The Brabbit family pushed through the crowded area, all of them filled with great anticipation. They had waited so long for this night. It had been back in the time of the summer goddess that Mr Brabbit had been killed, and this was the one night when they would get the chance to see him again and talk sense with him.

Like Dill's family, the Brabbits had been going through a dark time. It had lasted four months, and for rabbits that is a long time. Mrs Brabbit had blamed herself for the loss of her husband, as she hadn't seen the predator who had taken him in time to warn him to flee. It was making her feel so dark, and all of her bunnies were feeling her pain. But they knew that on a thin place like the hill of the fairies and at a thin time like the first night of the winter goddess, all those who had gone to Light Land could come back and bond with their loved ones for a short time and help them to understand that their light was still alive. It was nature's way of healing her creatures.

It was commonly understood here that every living creature had an inner body or light body inside their hard body, and when the hard body died, the light body went back to Light Land, which was where everybody came from in the first place. It was when the light body grew dim while still connected to the hard body that life began to be difficult and everyone connected to that person felt their sadness and pain. This was why Mrs Brabbit had to be on the hill of the fairies tonight: she had to make a connection with her partner's light body, which would reignite her own light body. Then she would be free of the dark time, as would her children. She had asked for this at the wish tree in the time of the autumn goddess, and her wish was about to be granted by the winter goddess, Cailasha.

A lot of mumbling was going on – hoots, growls, caws, tweets and squeaks – as everyone waited for proceedings to begin. This could only happen when the atmosphere became thin and the Lord of the Dells made his appearance.

The lord was the most magnificent animal in the dip 'n' dells; he was a huge white stag who stood taller than any other creature that occupied the area. His presence was awesome and every creature showed him the utmost respect. He presided over all of the four annual gatherings here in the dells and his word was law, of that there was no doubt. It was said that he was a gift from the goddesses and that his role was to make certain that all of the laws of nature were adhered to in the dip 'n' dells. It was also believed that he was the oldest animal still here in the hard body. Some even believed that he could raise his light so much that he could go in and out of Light Land without having to give up his hard body. What all the creatures were sure of was how majestic the lord was and how his light would expand to shine on every one of the creatures at these gatherings.

Mrs Brabbit had settled her family on one of the giant orange roots that extended from the base of the wish tree. Her eldest bunny, Jack, was standing up on his back legs and scanning the area for the predators who would normally want to eat him when he heard his mother say, 'Jack Brabbit, get down and be still.'

He did get down, but he was so excited, as were his two sisters, Bunty and Droopsy, who were both stretching out their necks to look over the heads of the adult hares who had leaped in front of them.

'I can't see, Mummy, I can't see past the two big ears,' Droopsy Brabbit was complaining.

'I can't see either,' Bunty moaned, sticking her twitchy nose up above her head with an air of superiority.

'Shushhhh, all of you, I've explained this to you already: you don't see with your eyes, you see sense.'

There was something final in the way Mrs Brabbit said this to her children, and it was understood in an instant. Calm descended on her small family.

Silence was also creeping over the crowd on the opposite side of the circle, like wind moving through a field of long grass. Mrs Brabbit could see a path opening up as all the ground creatures pushed into one another to create space for the great stag.

His footsteps could now be heard on the crisp hard ground and the first thing Mrs Brabbit could make out was his antlers coming into view. Then there he was, entering the circle.

Nothing seemed to move except the Lord of the Dells himself. Slowly, deliberately, after one long glance around the circle, he took his position beside the wish tree.

Even the wind fell at that moment, making it appear to the creatures gathered there that the lord had power over the elements. Maybe he did. He lifted his head and looked through the branches above him, following the shards of moonlight that were beginning to burst through the dense foliage of the wish tree. He opened his nostrils, drawing the night air deep into his lungs before exhaling a cloud of steamy breath from his mouth that sat for a second above Jack Brabbit's head. The little rabbit was hypnotised as he studied the patterns forming in the steam.

The stag sent out a feeling in the language of sense that every animal, bird, insect and reptile in the circle of trees instantly understood: 'Be still and bow your head in respect for the goddess Cailasha, for she is now the keeper of the sky.'

In the wintery mist above the dells a presence was building, and all at the gathering felt it. The frosted ground began to reflect the white moonlight all around the circle, making the trees look as though they were being up-lit for a great event.

The great stag gave out more sense: 'She is the winter goddess and she teaches us about life, death and rebirth in the world.'

The silence intensified and the frost sparkled.

'Nothing that lives can truly die,' said the stag, 'but we all must experience a winter in our lives, otherwise we haven't truly lived.'

The tone of this teaching was felt by each creature in its own way. It was the kind of teaching that was absorbed more than understood; it became part of you and even if you couldn't understand it at the moment when it was given, it would reveal itself to you when you needed it most.

'This is the time when things become slow, and they become slow in order for you to reflect on and learn from the times you have come through. Those of you who are in your first winter will learn that Cailasha allows you to rest and ponder, and when you rest and ponder, the light body grows, and as the light body grows, so does your sense.'

The stag's wide eyes took in the whole scene, and his heart was content, and all could feel it.

Another deep in-breath was followed by billows of steam as he raised his eyes to the sky, where Cailasha was waiting in cloud form to draw back the veil that separated the two worlds.

A high-pitched sound was now ringing out around the hill of the fairies, the light was neither night nor day, the ground was like the surface of the moon and all of life in the dip 'n' dells was connected and in complete harmony. Something special was happening, nothing was solid anymore, the place was thin and even the stillness had a kind of motion in it, flowing through the gathering like a wave. It was time.

Lights of all colours began to appear in the moonlit forest. Starting out like little pearls and fairy lights, they expanded until they looked like bubbles, clear and transparent but with rainbow light moving through them.

For the creatures who were less than a year old, this was the most amazing thing that had ever happened to them, and at some point they would drift off into a state of grace and peace, while the older ones who had been here before just went with the moment and accepted the gift of light from the goddess.

Some lights were guiding other lights to certain families. Each family who had lost a loved one in the last three seasons was given a ball of light, and in it was the light body of the one they had lost. For what felt like a second or a lifetime, they could see, hear and feel that family member once more and learn that the disconnection of death was only temporary and that all that was required to reunite loved ones on opposite sides of the veil was love itself.

Mrs Brabbit was embracing her husband, who was looking better than he ever had when he was in his hard body, she thought, and this was sense they were talking, which meant that she couldn't have private thoughts, but he just laughed and motioned all his family to come closer to him.

He told his wife that it wasn't her fault that he'd been taken and that she wasn't to worry, because death didn't hurt.

'It feels like a natural transition,' he said, 'and of course I still feel completely connected to you and the children. I can still see you and feel you – but you have enough sense to know that anyway, don't you?'

'Yes, I do now. I can really feel it.'

Mrs Brabbit's light was shining out in all directions, she was so happy to have this moment with her husband. Her children stayed silent, but were all moved by the experience.

'I'm in Light Land,' Mr Brabbit told them, 'but I won't miss a moment of your lives. I love you all and always will, my darling family.'

For Mrs Brabbit and her bunnies, it was such a comfort to know that their father would see them grow up and hear them when they needed him and know when they did well. Nothing, he told them, would be missed, and he told his wife that he would always be there for her and that one day they would be together again in a world where nothing could die and no one could ever separate them again.

These joyous moments lifted mother and children to the point where they were glowing in an iridescent blue light and there were tears of happiness all round.

Mr Brabbit also had to name the predator who taken his life, and that predator would have to go before the stag at the next gathering, in the springtime, to receive his predator's pardon. This was part of the natural law of this place. Taking a life was the worst offence a creature could commit here, unless it was done out of hunger or true need. Then and only then would the beast be given a chance to appeal for a predator's pardon and natural forgiveness would take place. Any other reason for taking a life was completely unacceptable and it would be left to the goddess of the season to deal with whoever had done such a terrible thing.

It was no surprise to Mrs Brabbit that the predator who had taken her husband was a fox named Jonnie, as he was always hanging around their home. He would have to face the stag at the next gathering.

Life for the Brabbits would now go back to normal. Better still, light would return to their mother and to their lives in general.

The gathering drew to a close, but even after it had ended no one moved for a while as there was still such a spectacle of light around the wish tree that everyone felt compelled to be there and bathe in the beauty and love that were in the air.

'There is much to be discussed tomorrow,' Mrs Brabbit thought, and her bunnies nodded in agreement, but for now they would all just stay and enjoy the love and magic that the goddess and the little light fairies had given them.

Grandma and Dill were still standing looking at the moon, which now seemed to be sitting directly on top of the wish tree. The old lady pulled her blanket tight around her shoulders, although Dill's big tartan blanket was hanging loosely as though he wasn't aware of the winter chill.

Frost was sparkling in the moonlight, and around the hill of the fairies, lights were twinkling like the fairy lights on a Christmas tree. Dill looked up at his grandma and saw that she had tears running down her face, but she was smiling, even glowing with a white light.

She leaned down, pulled him closer to her and whispered, 'Isn't it magic, Dill?'

'Why are you crying when you're happy, Grandma?'

'Do you know why, Dill? Because I know that everything's going to be alright now, just wait and see.'

The old lady snapped her fingers to call Bramble and in an instant the dog jumped onto the wall beside them and became part of a group hug beneath the blankets. Dill felt a sense of lightness and contentment building between them all.

The moon had moved past the wish tree now and the light was leaving the hill of the fairies. The scene that had been so bright a moment ago was now in shadow. Night had truly fallen and tomorrow something new would begin.

Chapter Six
Sense and Sense-ability

Jack Brabbit was bouncing around the little mounds of earth next to his home, which was in a hole in the ground underneath a deformed hawthorn tree and a big gorse bush behind the back left corner of the garden at Moon Cottage. He was full of beans after the gathering at the thin place by the wish tree, as were all his family, but Jack had only one way of displaying his happiness, and that was to run, bounce and leap until he had exhausted the abundance of energy that filled his young body.

He was still on the alert, though. His mother had warned him about the dog that lived in the cottage and told him to be careful because even though it had some sense, it was also very unpredictable and they didn't know its routine.

Jack had learned so much about predators' routines from his mother; she was adept when it came to escaping them. The first thing she had taught him was: 'The best way not to get caught is not to be there.' Jack loved that. His mother had more sense than any other rabbit in the land. She taught her brood when to feed and where, and when it was safest to come out to play in the dells. Her awareness of the times and places predators hunted was second to none. Yes, she was full of sense, and now that she had her light back, her sense was through the roof.

Jack's mother was almost 17 goddesses old, and that was quite something for a dells rabbit. She was considered very bright among the rabbit community and she always told her son that he had her light and that he would be very special someday. But for now he was still little

Jack Brabbit and he was bouncing through the lumpy, bumpy ground close to his home.

He stopped for a breather under the garden wall in the tunnel that led to the human place. It was one of the safest places for the Brabbits to go because not many animals had ventured there since the humans had come back.

Jack was very intelligent for a young rabbit, but that also meant that he could be quite inquisitive and he often found himself being drawn to things he had been told not to go near. One of the things he was fascinated by was the small human. He had even got very close to him once at the stone circle. He had a strong feeling that he was like the old woman. He knew she could talk sense and he could see that they both had strong light bodies.

His mother was interested in the humans too. She made all the Brabbits go into the garden of Moon Cottage at night before the owls came out and do sendings for them. Sendings were something that dells creatures did for other families after they had lost a loved one and before they could go to a thin place to take part in a gathering. Mrs Brabbit had told all her family to send a request to the goddess to help the humans find their light, because since their arrival the cottage had become very dim.

Jack wanted to know why his mother was so keen for them to help the humans, but she told him that he should trust her because she could feel that it was the right thing to do.

The human boy was sitting in the garden now, quite close to the tunnel where Jack was resting. He was reading a book and Jack could see the pictures that were forming in his mind. Some creatures could hear what others were thinking and feeling, while others could see what was going on in their mind, and Jackie-boy could do both. His mother could do even better: she had the very rare ability to see, hear *and* know, which was the strongest measure of sense there was. She had always told him that one day he would inherit this ability.

The boy was looking at pictures of birds in his book. He gave off a feeling of being quite contented, Jack thought. Then he got a picture of a huge fat bird with long legs and a long neck with a small head on the top of it. This was like nothing the young rabbit had ever known and he couldn't help laughing at it. But he soon stopped when he saw the boy look his way and heard him say, 'It's not that funny.'

Dill knew that something was watching him from the tunnel because his stomach told him so. But what was it?

'I won't harm you,' he felt like saying, and even without the words coming out of his mouth, he knew that his observer had understood what he was feeling.

Jack's curiosity was pulling him towards the boy, but he remembered he had to be careful. 'What if the big dog is there?' he said to himself.

'No, she's out with my grandma. Oh, did I just say that?' Dill wondered.

Jack couldn't wait – his back legs shot him forwards almost involuntarily.

The boy gave out a feeling of great joy. It was a rabbit who was speaking to him!

'You did just say that,' Jack told him. 'You can talk sense then. Mummy says that I have lots of sense and that I will keep getting better at it. I just know things sometimes as well. I know that you won't harm me, because I can feel it.'

Dill took a moment to catch what the rabbit was communicating, as it was coming at him so quickly, but then his inner voice took over and he replied, 'Yes, I can talk sense, but only sometimes. More when I'm not in the house, and lots when I'm with my grandma and with Bramble, especially when we're playing together by the stones.'

In that short exchange Jack had seen the inside of the cottage and knew that the grandma was the old woman and that Bramble was the big crazy dog. He felt excited and his light got brighter.

Dill could feel it too. He wanted to ask the bunny where he came from and whether he was hungry, but a feeling came back at him: 'Stop calling me "bunny", my name is Jack Brabbit and I'm two and a bit goddesses old.'

Now it was Dill's turn to laugh.

'Why is that funny?' Jack sent out.

'Because,' Dill sent back, 'I've never actually spoken to a rabbit before. And it's just so funny that you have a name.'

'Why? Don't you have a name? My mummy calls you "the small human".'

'My name is Dillan, but everybody calls me Dill.'

Dill? Jack felt so much laughter bursting through him that he did a kind of flip into the air with his back legs, then span round quickly three times.

Oh! This was all just sooo funny! Dill dropped to his knees with laughter and his book went flying into the air.

The thud of the book hitting the ground stopped Jack's laughter instantly. He froze for a second before shooting back into the tunnel and doing a quick half-spin to face Dill again from the safety of his hiding-place.

Dill wasn't laughing either.

'I'm really, really sorry, Jack,' his heart was saying to the rabbit as he slowly approached the tunnel on his hands and knees. When his nose was right in front of the entrance, he sat back on his heels, hoping that he hadn't scared Jack away.

But the little rabbit had understood. He popped back out into the garden and sat in front of Dill's knees, his ears folded on his back, staring up at him with big dark eyes.

As they gazed at each other something in the light around both of them changed: the white luminous glow turned golden. At that moment a connection was made between them and joy filled both their light bodies.

Dill lowered his hand softly onto the rabbit's back. He had found a new friend.

After that, every day at around the same time Dill sat by the tunnel and waited for Jack to come out. They loved being together and they couldn't hide anything from each other when they talked sense. The rabbit taught Dill how to use it in ways that even his grandma didn't know. He taught him how to sense danger by paying attention to the flutters in his stomach and said that it was important to trust his light body and to let it guide him to what he needed. He made Dill aware that the things he needed could be very different from the things he wanted.

'Things we want come from the hard body; things we need are told to us by the light body,' he said in a very strict tone, which Dill immediately knew came from Mrs Brabbit, as he picked up Jack's memory of learning it from her.

'Wow.' He shook his head in amazement as he felt the expansion of his own sense.

'Yeah, it's great, isn't it? I just got what you got, only I got understanding with it too.' Jack was beaming.

Dill loved their time together, only he had to make sure that Bramble wasn't there, as he instinctively knew that she could hurt Jack without intending to. But for some reason his grandma had started to take the dog for very long walks around the time Dill was thinking about meeting his chum, and even when they returned, they entered the house through the front door rather than the back garden. There was something about this that made Dill feel sure that his grandmother knew about his friendship with Jack and was happy for him – well, that's what his sense was telling him.

Dill was sitting in a corner of the garden one day with the little rabbit by his side. It had been a strange six weeks or so since Halloween, he thought. He and Jack had shared their different experiences of the night when Cailasha had come to the hill of the fairies. Dill had remembered his grandma's tears of happiness and how she'd told him that things were going to be alright, and the young rabbit had searched his deepest feelings and nodded in agreement.

Since that night Dill's parents had lightened a little, even though they weren't surrounded by light like his grandmother and Bramble, and certainly not like Jack, but his stomach told him that there was still something heavy around the corner. When he told Jack about it, the rabbit gave a little shudder, which told Dill he was right.

His little friend moved onto his lap, trying to explain what his parents might be feeling. He told Dill how dim their light bodies were.

'They gave so much of their light to your sister that they are empty now of good feelings, you see?'

It made sense to Dill that good feelings were associated with light, because he already knew that when he saw strong light glowing around people it was coming from the happiness inside them.

Jack had confirmed this in earlier exchanges of sense. He'd told Dill about his own mother and how her light had almost gone out after his father had been taken by the predator and how it had affected all of his family. He knew that what Dill wanted more than anything else in the world was for his parents to get their own light back. It was more than a want, it was a need.

'Look,' he told him, 'my sisters and I felt the same need for our mother to get better when Father was taken. Even though we were so young, her feelings affected us too. Rabbit families play a lot together and not to have that contact when we are young can really affect us when we are older.'

He continued the story of his family's dark time. Mrs Brabbit's light body had been so low at times that she had had to stay in the burrow.

'The hard body,' Jack said, 'has very little sense when the light body is drained, so if she had gone out, she could have acted without sense and been taken away from us too. All of us had to try to share our light with her to give her the strength to find sense again.'

As he spoke, Dill realised why his mother hadn't left the house much when his sister had died and why his grandma very rarely went into the dells with him and Bramble – her inner light was exhausted too.

Dill loved seeing the pictures in his friend's mind when they talked sense now, and he really loved the pictures of Jack's father coming back through the bubble of light on the night of the gathering. The heaven he was in seemed an amazing place, much happier than the place Amber had gone to; nothing about his parents' explanation had light in it. Only his grandma made heaven sound like Light Land.

It was amazing for Dill to hear that all the creatures around him had to deal with death and dying and that Mother Nature took care of their feelings in her own way by bringing change into their lives through the four seasons. Jack told him that the more he could understand change, the more he would understand life, and that when he understood the nature of his hard body, which was about a beginning and an end, he could get on with enjoying the part in between.

Snuggled up beside the garden wall, the two friends shared the deepest parts of their lives with each other. They both felt so safe in the uninterrupted exchange of energy that neither had any idea that they were being watched. Mrs Brabbit's head was poking out of the tunnel, while Dill's grandma looked on from the kitchen window. The older ladies were aware of each other, but kept still so as not to disturb the children's communication. And both had tears in their eyes, but neither was sad.

Chapter Seven
Beneath the Surface

They sky hung heavy and low over the land in the early hours of Christmas morning and Cailasha knew that the sheet of frost she had laid down on her arrival now needed to be replaced, so she took her giant staff and struck the frozen ground hard, knowing that the sound would vibrate and bring down the mighty blanket of snow she had been preparing over the past weeks. This was her gift to the land, an insulator that would also nourish all that was growing beneath the surface and protect it from the icy north winds that would follow.

Cailasha was the oldest and wisest of the goddesses. She was like a grandmother: she had seen much and knew how to behave appropriately in situations. She was wise enough to know that sometimes things had to be difficult if Earth's creatures were to learn and grow. Her season was clear and crisp, cold and sharp sometimes, but there was always a point to what she delivered in her time as guardian of the sky. Each goddess brought her own qualities to the dells and each had a teaching; the old lady's teachings were about survival, resilience and challenge, and her next challenge was to bring the sky down to meet the Earth.

Dill was woken by an almighty thud that seemed to make the entire house shake. He could hear his grandma walking around downstairs and his parents hurrying down to join her. Bramble shot off the bed, pulled the door back with her nose and tore downstairs also.

Dill was sitting up, about to get out of bed, when he looked out of the window. Instantly he threw back his covers and ran downstairs as well, shouting, 'Snow! Snow! It's snowing!'

Grandma was in the kitchen, reminding his father that she'd said it would come like this, and his father was standing at the window, rubbing his head in disbelief at the massive amount of snow that had dropped from the sky.

'Does it always happen like this? Wow, this is mad, isn't it?'

He looked around the room for agreement.

Dill's mother was already putting logs on the fire and he could hear the kettle boiling in the background, so he knew that they were all going to stay up, even though the clock on the wall only said 6.30.

His grandma was the first to greet him properly: 'Merry Christmas, Dill!'

In the excitement of the snow everyone had forgotten that it was Christmas morning. Dill's mother came over and hugged him, and his father did the same, and then all three adults stood back and looked at each other.

His father was the first to speak. 'Haven't you seen what's at the bottom of your bed, Dillan?'

'Eh? No, but, oh my God...'

He was bounding upstairs at 100 miles an hour. There were two pillowcases stuffed with gifts wrapped in colourful Christmas paper. Dill shouted out excitedly every time he ripped one open.

Meanwhile, before a present had been opened between them, his parents were out in the garden clearing a path through the snow to the shed where they kept the logs and a separate path for the dog to get out.

Dill came out and began to help his father make a snowman. There was so much snow that it didn't take long, but Bramble began to tear it down each time they got ready to put on the head.

Dill thought the dip ''n' dells looked amazing under snow. They reminded him of round buns covered with runny white icing.

His father was laughing hard as he chucked snowballs for Bramble to catch. Though she was disappearing under the snow from time to time, she was truly in her element. The joy they shared that morning was as bright as the snowy white landscape.

Dill loved his presents, especially his very first computer, which his father set up in his bedroom. The house was feeling light again and all of the family seemed as bright as they had on Halloween, but by late afternoon Dill could feel that his mother's heart was as heavy as the snow that was hanging off the roof of the cottage. He tried to keep her spirits high by telling her how much he loved everything she'd given him.

'I'm so glad, Dill. I love it that you love everything,' she said whilst chewing what looked like that last part of the little nail on her left hand. It was their first Christmas without Amber.

Suddenly he realised that in all the excitement of the day he'd forgotten about Jack. Was his family alright with all the heavy snow? Where they trapped in their burrow? A feeling of dread ran through him as he headed for the back door and put on his boots and coat to dig away the snow from the wall where they met.

Out in the garden, he was surprised to see that there was already a space cleared around the wall where the tunnel was, but he instantly knew that his grandma had done it, as a picture of it flashed into his mind. He felt better when he saw carrots scattered at the entrance of the hole too, and he could just make out a little shape in the dark space that appeared to be munching on the food. It was his little friend, and it felt good to know that he was safe and well.

Jack popped his head out of the tunnel.

'Hi, Dill, tell your grandma that we all said thanks for the grub,' he said through a mouthful of munched-up carrot, but he was talking sense, so it didn't matter that he was eating at the time.

He told him that his mother had known about the snow for ages and had told them all to stay in the burrow before it came down.

'Anyway, rabbits are great at digging tunnels in the ground, so this stuff is easy-peasy.'

Jack was giving off a feeling of happiness that made Dill smile. He stepped down into the clear space by the wall and crouched beside his little friend, gently stroking his long ears. Jack kicked out his back legs in response.

'Merry Christmas, Jack.'

The rabbit laughed, as he instantly understood that this was a happy day for humans.

Inside the cottage there was a very different feeling at that moment. As soon as Dill had left the house his mother had burst into a flood of tears.

His father tried to comfort her. 'I know she's not here. Just let it go.'

'How can you be so strong and I can't?' she cried. 'I really want to move on, but there is something, and I don't know what it is, and no one can help me, maybe because I'm weak or...'

Her husband held her tightly, feeling her sobs. They seemed to touch him somewhere that made him want to cry too.

'I want her back as well,' he said. 'I really miss her so much, but I have to try for Dill...'

'You both do.'

Grandma joined them, hugging them both and fighting off the tears that were stuck in her own throat.

'It wouldn't be normal if you didn't feel like this today. You'd be heartless not to miss your daughter on Christmas Day. Please, don't be hard on yourselves. It's still early – only half a year has gone past. The boy is outside, he's OK, and you need to do this, but let's all try and help each other to be strong.'

Grandma's words seemed to have a healing effect on both Dill's parents. They hugged each other even more tightly for a moment and then breathed deeply together before letting each other go and heading to different parts of the kitchen.

Dill entered the house with a warm glow around him, but his mood changed when he noticed that his mother had been crying and there was a cold feeling coming from his father. He knew that they had been sad again, but he had expected that. He'd known they would find it hard today without Amber.

Last year, Dill remembered, they'd all gone to have their Christmas dinner with his sister in the hospital. There had been lots of families of sick children gathered round the table. Amber had been too ill to sit at the table, but they had all sat round her bed and opened presents for her before they had gone to eat.

He suddenly felt very sorry for his parents and instinctively walked over to his mother and gave her a very tight hug. His father came across to join in. Dill held both parents and tried to give his light to them, and it seemed to work, because his mother began to laugh. She kissed both her men on the cheek, then broke away and said, 'Right, it's Christmas and we need to have some fun. Who's for games?'

She had drawn a strength from her son that made her pick herself up, push her hair back from her wet cheeks and tuck it behind both ears at the same time. Even her voice became strong and solid.

'Let's get the Monopoly, shall we?'

They sat round the big kitchen table playing board games for the rest of the evening in a kind of awkward happiness.

The snow lasted through most of the month of January and was accompanied by some of the coldest winds imaginable. The weather had closed in as Dill's grandma had told them it would. She knew this place and in her wisdom had made his parents fill the big freezer in the back porch, because the roads leading to Moon Cottage would be out of use for some time.

The winter reminded Dill of how his parents were feeling. The earth was being held down and things appeared normal, but all the while there were other things happening underneath. Things that had been there before were preparing to come forth again and new things were going to appear that hadn't been there at all. He knew that their sadness would come back again, but he hoped that they might find new feelings to replace it or to help them fight it. Could Mother Nature heal their grief? How could that happen?

He hoped that when the new goddess burst through the ground with her feisty energy the sadness would burst out of his parents. The way he sensed it was that the sadness was being kept prisoner inside both of them and it wanted to be released, but by letting it go they felt they would be betraying his sister in some way.

Then he wondered if it was the other way around: that the sadness was keeping them prisoner and denying them happiness, because if they were happy that would also be in some way a betrayal of his sister. But that would mean that they were being punished, and he knew that they had done nothing but love his sister, so how could that be?

Dill decided to stop thinking for now and go and play in the garden. It wouldn't be long before the snow was gone, as the branches on the trees and bushes were brown now, and standing out in sharp contrast to the ground around them.

Bramble was itching to go outside too. Dill knew this because her small docked tail was moving from side to side over the back porch floor in the same way that the windscreen wipers did on the car when it was wet.

'Come on then – let's go out, girl,' he said loudly, yanking open the big wooden door and letting the dog burst free.

'At last! I thought you were never going to open that door!' she screamed out in her best sense.

The boy laughed out loud to the empty sky around him.

'You are a mad dog, Brams, but I love you,' he called out, not knowing if it came in words or sense.

In the week that followed, rain came to the dells and the temperature rose slightly. Warmer winds began to blow up from the south-west, and though Cailasha did her best to hold the land under the grasp of winter, she was tiring fast. The snow had completely melted by the last day of the month and her friend the north wind had nothing left to blow. The thick cloud that blocked the sun was starting to break up and the ground was covered with puddles and patches of water. The little lake had grown somewhat as the snows had melted and now looked like huge mirror on the land, reflecting the hill of the fairies, at whose foot it lay.

There was definitely a change in the air. Clouds were moving in all directions as if they were looking for a place to go, while the land seemed to be moving with the promise of something magnificent about to happen. The space between land and sky was once again becoming thin.

Standing at the stones, as they had the day before the last changeover, Dill and his grandmother could feel the wrestling match going on as the incoming goddess claimed the keep of the land and sky from her predecessor.

This was a different battle from the last one. That had taken place in the sky, but this felt as though something from above was sucking something up from the ground like a great vacuum cleaner. A freezing wind caused small puddles to turn to ice and then warmer breezes brought a strange vapour into the atmosphere, making a foggy mist rise above the land. The atmosphere became thick and hazy, and in the fading light of dusk Dill and his grandma could just make out a large misty cloud formation to the right of the hill of the fairies. It was the form of the winter goddess.

She didn't look as strong or as proud as when they had seen her three months ago; now her hair was hanging all around her and her body was bent and frail. She looked exhausted, but she would wait like this until Brigisha claimed the land, and that wouldn't happen until the place was thin enough.

Grandma said, 'Now, Dill, before she leaves we must thank Cailasha for watching over us. The poor thing has given her all.'

'Goodbye, Cailasha,' Dill called out to the sky. He waved his hand to the goddess.

He wanted to stay longer and see Brigisha burst through the land, but his grandma gave him one of her knowing looks and said, 'You won't see Brigisha tonight, Dill, but I assure you that by morning you will know she has arrived.'

Dill felt sad for a moment as the old lady started to fade, but in an instant the feeling was replaced by the thought that she wasn't dead or dying, she was just changing. Dill liked that thought; it made him stand up straight and tall. His grandma put her arm on his shoulder and pulled him close to her. Standing there together, they shared a moment of sense that made the grandmother feel ten years old and the boy feel old and wise.

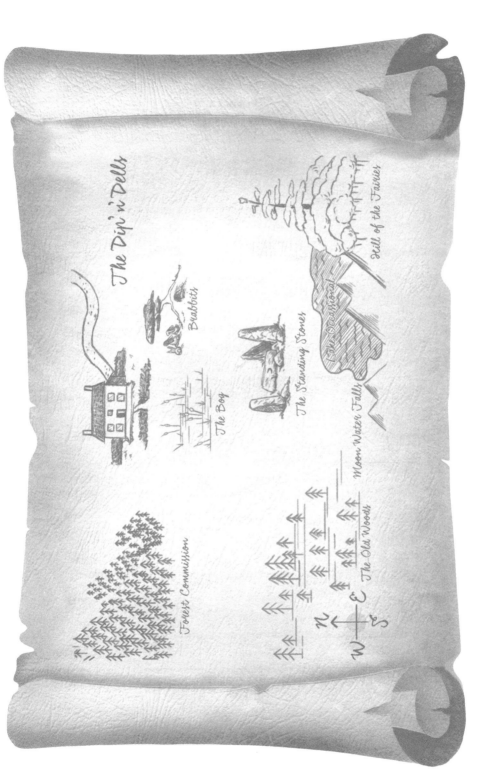

The Dip'n'Dells

Brabbith

The Bog

Forest Commission

The Standing Stones

Moon Water Falls

The Old Woods

The Occasional

Hill of the Fairies

N W E S

Chapter Eight
The Predators' Pardon

The footsteps running over the soft damp ground make squidgy sounds – squish, squish, squish... And the smell – yes, the air is perfumed with the newness of plant life. Sweet yet sticky, pungent but indulgent, it makes me want to drag it into my body to feel a part of the world around me.

I am heading to a gathering of people – well, animals who are like people. They are my people and they accept me. Grams is taking me to them. She is so happy, I am happy and the countryside is alive and I can feel it, I am part of it. The excitement is as heavy as the perfumed air. Keep running – I must run faster. Squish, splash, squish, splash...

I am stopping. It's amazing, all these lights with little people in them, smiling at me. They are happy to see me and my heart is bursting with joy to see them.

My friends are here. Rowena, my best friend, the most beautiful creature I have ever seen, she is a young deer, golden brown with large round eyes like deep pools of enticing liquid. It is the spring gathering in the old wood and I am there with Rowena and the others. Ah...

The light is coming up over the hill, and how magnificent the wish tree looks – still green, evergreen, it is the one thing that never changes. It is a still point amid the motion of life. The light is golden and alive, and she is there, the girl is in the sky and I can see her, she is...

'Oh!' She was sitting bolt upright in bed, facing her bedroom window. 'That was some dream.'

She turned sideways, then shuffled to the edge of the bed to put her feet down on the cold wooden floor and ground herself in reality.

Her eyes hadn't quite opened yet and she pondered for a moment on what had just happened. It wasn't really a dream, she knew, but a memory of her childhood in the dells. The thought of it brought warmth to her body and she remained sitting there for a moment to allow more memories to come to her.

Grandma hadn't relived such memories for a long time and she decided to indulge herself a little while longer, as no one in the house had stirred yet.

The stillness of the chilly bedroom made it easy to return to a cool day in the dip 'n' dells. It was the last time she'd attended a gathering, at the age of 13. Her parents were taking her to live in the city and it seemed to her that it wasn't just summer that was over but her whole childhood. It was the first day of the autumn goddess, which that year was at the end of July. The seasons in the dells had no real resemblance to the outside world, and even though the change of the goddesses took place at roughly the same time each year, it was Mother Nature who decided it. Only when she had chosen the day would the goddess appear, and that could be anytime, late or early.

I can see the standing stones clearly now – the mood stones, Grams calls them, but Rowena says they are really called the moon stones. The gathering is taking place there.

All of the creatures are there. The golden eagle who is the Lord of the Dells is descending from the sky to sit on the top of the tallest stone. Lights are appearing around him, and around all the creatures.

Ercesha appears in the sky, lights a torch from the setting sun and makes the clouds burn orange and red. It has been a chilly day, the chilliest day of summer, and thunder has been heard in the dells. It is said that Ercesha makes that noise to wake up the slumbering summer goddess and warn her that her time is over.

The clouds have cleared now, save for a few that look like candy floss.

They are pink, red, orange and bronze. It is a magical spectacle...

All my fears about what lies ahead in my new life are leaving me now.

Later the eagle has a message for me alone: 'This is not the end of your life, but merely the ending of a season. You will see many autumns in your life, in many different places. The time of Ercesha is about collecting what is available to help you in the future, so gather all that you have amassed from this special place, store it in your heart and let it sustain you through your life. Take your knowledge and use it in your new world to help people and allow them to wake up to this world, the real world.'

'Aahhh...' So real was the memory that the words caused her to rock backwards, as they had on the evening they were spoken to her.

Now she was back in the dells, her mind was so clear that her sense was coming back to her more and more. She was able to use it with Dill and the dog, and she had even used it with Mrs Brabbit, unbeknown to Dill or Jack. She needed a voice like Mrs Brabbit's in the animal world if she was to get help for the family, but she had been trying to keep herself to herself as much as possible until she could be sure that she could put a plan in motion.

Suddenly she was truly awake. 'OK, old girl, time to face the day head on and spring into action!'

She bounced from the bed to her feet and in one motion stretched out her arms, pulled open the curtains and allowed the room to be filled with light.

It was the first day of spring and as far as the eye could see the land had been set free of winter. There had been an explosion of green over the bumpy hills, and though there were no actual leaves on the trees, they were standing proud, waiting to be dressed in their new foliage. The light was different also: there was a sharpness that made each individual tree, plant, bush and rock look clear and defined. All sorts of plants had burst through the earth, and though still in tight bud, they gave off the sense that they were getting ready to take part in a great show.

Dill had dreamed that there was a warm wind blowing over the landscape very close to the ground. It moved swiftly yet silently, caressing every dip and dell like a blind hand feeling its way across a new environment. For a moment he thought he could see a young girl appear and then disappear. Was it his sister? But no, Amber was sick and couldn't move that speedily. Then he realised that it was the spring goddess, Brigisha. She looked so like his sister, with her curly blonde hair, only her energy was fast and powerful. How could she be so powerful, she was only a young girl – but no, she represented youth itself... His dream led him off at high speed to the old wood, where he talked to animals and birds, and Jack was with him, and Grandma...

When he woke, he couldn't wait to get out into the garden. There seemed to be a quickening in the air that had been missing in the time of Cailasha. Maybe it was because there were birds everywhere, tweeting and chirping as they swooped up and down over the land and back into the air in some sort of ritual dance. And the first sound he heard was the call of the cuckoo. His grandma had told him that he would know spring by that one particular call from the woods. She said that the cuckoo was as difficult to see as the spring goddess herself, but its call was unmistakable and told all the other creatures that it was the first day of the new season.

Dill smiled, and that smile wasn't just on his face, it was coming from deep inside him.

'What you grinning at, mate?' Jack Brabbit called out from under the garden wall.

'Jack, you're out early today. Is it OK for you to be here now? Won't you be in danger from predators?'

'No, today is the first day of the goddess and it is a thin time, so predators can't harm me now. I thought you knew that, Dill. Not even your mad crazy hound can touch me today!'

'What do you mean? Who told you this? Oh, do you want to meet her then? She's really nice,' Dill was stumbling over his words in his excitement at the thought of Jack and Bramble together.

'Oi, one thing at a time!' the little rabbit cried. 'Give me a chance and I'll tell you about it. Remember back when I told you about the winter gathering?'

Dill nodded slowly. He did remember, but there had been so much to digest about that gathering…

'OK, you don't totally remember. I get it, chum, this is sense and you're not so on the ball yet that you can hide things from me. OK, on the first day of any goddess, no predators must hunt, kill or eat their prey. *To do so would be catastrophic to their entire species.* Don't ask me what that means, but that's what the stag says, and my mum.'

Jack paused for a moment to let his friend take in what he had shared with him.

He went on, 'Your dog does have some sense, so even she will know inside herself that she can't harm a fly today. And the reason I know all this, well, it's because I'm a very clever rabbit and, eh, my mum reminded me of it this morning.'

Jack had an impish glow about him today, Dill thought. He was fascinated by what he had said and had many other questions for him, but the little rabbit was so excited he had to carry on, and Dill could feel this too, so he sat patiently and listened to his friend.

'This evening as the sun goes down there is the spring gathering. It's in the old wood this time. That is a thin place, like the hill of the fairies. But while Cailasha's gathering is about life and death and Light Land, Brigisha's gathering is about justice and balance and letting go of things that hurt us or hold us back. Brigisha makes us look at what we've come through and pay for it, or deal with it, but she gives us new things as well, to remind us that what made us dark is in the past. She can offer us more light and sustenance to begin again. Everything in her time is about renewal and starting things from fresh.'

Dill wished that his parents could be allowed to go to the gathering in the old wood and let go of their hurts and pains and become a normal family that played and talked a lot, like Jack's family. After all, the Brabbits had come through a dark time when his father was taken and after the winter gathering they had got their light back.

Jack understood his friend's feelings; he could see every thought in Dill's mind and wanted so much to help him.

'Things will change, Dill,' he said quietly.

Still, he had a strong instinct that that wasn't going to happen tonight. He wondered if Dill could sense this, so changed his mood quickly.

'I know, why don't you come to the gathering? You can hide at the edge of the wood and maybe you'll get answers or something.'

'Yes, maybe in all the sense that is shared, I'll hear what I need to hear to help Mum and Dad.'

For a moment they both had a vision of Dill at the gathering. They didn't know if they were imagining it or creating it, but it lifted both their light bodies to a new height.

Then the back door opened slowly and both Jack and Dill could sense his grandma coming out. 'Now, wait,' they heard her say and they both knew that she was addressing Bramble, who was waiting patiently behind the door, sitting perfectly still like a good girl, except for the little tail that was sweeping across the floor, from side to side, at 100 miles an hour.

'Come, slowly, slowly,' Grandma was commanding.

Dill was astounded to see how well his dog was following the orders; normally she burst out of the house and span round like a fiend before tearing off over the garden wall.

'Now, sit' was the next command, and Bramble sat with her ears pulled back from the side of her head, looking like she did when Dill's mother scolded her for stealing from the kitchen table.

'Now stay, Bramble, there's a good girl,' Grandma said in an affectionate tone that made the dog drop her head and look upwards with big eyes that said, 'Love me.'

Grandma looked over in Dill's direction and said, 'Don't be afraid, Jack, you can come out a little at a time. I think this is as good a time as any for you to get to know Bramble. After all, she is your neighbour.'

Dill was amazed. His grandma seemed to know who Jack was, and his name, and that the dog couldn't hurt him today. And it felt as though Bramble was connected to her in the same way that he and Jack were connected.

'Now, remember, Jack,' she continued, 'this is her first time meeting someone like you, and she is very nervous, so be gentle with her. She won't hurt you, I promise.'

Dill was thrilled. He missed not playing with Bramble when he had his talks with Jack and he didn't like his two best friends not being allowed to meet. He also had many questions for his grandmother, as did Jack, but in an instant the old lady sent out a sense message to both of them: 'In time, little ones, in time.'

The intensity in the small corner of the garden grew as the dog almost crawled towards Jack, measuring each inch, so mindful to contain her usual force that it felt as though she was moving in slow motion towards the timid little creature.

As she crept along she made little soft slurping noises with her velvet lips, which came out in the language of sense as 'Hi, eh, hello, eh, eh, I'm, I'm, eh.'

'Don't be shy now. Just be careful, like I taught you, girl,' Grandma instructed the bashful dog.

In an effort to make her feel more at ease, Jack made a small move forward, which brought his nose up to the same level as the dog's, and they sniffed in each other's scent. In an instant there was a connection between them.

It wasn't long before Bramble was feeling confident enough to stand up tall and even give Jack a half-crinkle. That made him bounce round in circles laughing, because in sense it translated into laughter. Dill and his grandma joined in, and the light in this corner of the garden grew stronger until it became a very bright place to be.

Grandma had prepared the dog for this moment for some time now, along with Mrs Brabbit, who had become her secret friend. Now the old lady sent a knowing look towards the tunnel under the wall and an adult rabbit nodded in return.

The first day of spring was always bright in the dells. There was something rousing about knowing you could let go of the past and make a positive new start. All the creatures appreciated the chance to move forward without the weight of past pain, guilt and sadness. Even the predators showed this, like the buzzards circling on extended wings with finger-like feathers open at the ends, presenting their gold and orangey-brown plumage to the sun in honour of the goddess of springtime.

Dill was watching the large birds of prey from the kitchen window.

'It must be amazing to be that high above the world. Maybe they're the eyes of the goddesses, reporting what they see. Maybe when we see these birds we could look down on our lives too, see them from a higher perspective. That could be an idea…?'

He was thinking out loud, but no one could hear him, not because there wasn't anyone there, but because they were talking to each other on a different frequency from him.

'Look, I'll talk to you in the car, just let me get my things together and we can try to have a rational conversation.'

Dill's mother was chewing her nails at the same time as she speaking to his father.

'Yes, I hear you,' he said impatiently, 'but if we don't get started, we'll never get anything done and you know we need supplies.'

He shrugged.

'Oh, whatever… Do what you want.'

Grandma came into the kitchen, smiling one of her warm smiles and holding two frozen pizzas in her hands.

'Found two more, my boy, so we are in luck today, thank the goddess.'

Both his parents turned to look at her as she plodded across the kitchen, not seeming to notice the atmosphere and actually whistling a tune.

As she looked back at them with a soft smile on her face, it had the effect of a quiet slap. Both seemed to snap out of their bickering and gather themselves together.

'Vi, you will make sure he reads and goes to bed at a reasonable time tonight?'

'Of course.'

'And, Mother, can you leave out some bread so it is ready by morning? It will be too late when we get back.'

'Of course, dear. Now you two need to get going, and please try to relax and have a good time. Remember it's the first day of spring.'

Dill's parents looked at each other with quizzical expressions on their faces. It was nowhere near the first day of spring in the world they belonged to. Concern for the older woman made them forget what they'd been fighting about earlier. They left the house a little uncertainly, glancing back at Dill and his grandmother, who were having a great time preparing dinner in the kitchen and laughing with the dog, who was now standing on her hind legs at the table beside them.

Dusk was approaching by the time Dill and his grandmother had finished eating their supper. Dill was feeling heavy after the large amount of pizza he had eaten, and his mind was feeling heavy too. He knew why – it was because his parents seemed to be the only two living creatures in the dip 'n' dells that didn't feel how light the day had been. They weren't unhappy as much these days, but they didn't appear to notice how beautiful and magical life was. They were missing everything around them because they very seldom left the house, and when they were in it they were nearly always apart, as his father spent almost all day in his little office upstairs and his mother seemed confined to the kitchen. Maybe the trip to town would help them, he thought. His grandma had booked them a table at the one restaurant the small town had to offer.

'OK,' she said, and she was talking in sense now that they had the house to themselves. He could feel that she wanted to tell him something, and she became aware that he knew it. With her little knowing smile, she said, in words this time, 'Alright, I have to take you somewhere this evening. Now, please listen carefully to what I say. It is important, Dillan.'

Excitement ran through his entire body because he knew what was coming, and even though she was speaking out loud, he could hear it, feel it and see it all at the same time: she was taking him to the thin place tonight, to the gathering of all the dells creatures. His mind began to race. He would get to meet Jack's sisters, and see the Lord of the Dells, and all the animals and birds he'd watched from a distance would be right up close to him…

'Stop!' Grandma said, in a stricter tone than he'd expected. 'Dill, I really need you to listen to me.'

She told him that as his parents were away for the rest of the night and she needed to be at the gathering, he had to go too. She had cleared it for him to be there.

He started to wonder why she had to be there, but she simply said, 'All will be explained later. But you are free to join Mrs Brabbit and her family and watch the proceedings with all the other creatures.'

As she spoke, he caught a quick flash of her with a lady rabbit. They were talking sense and Bramble was with them. But no sooner had he received this than his grandmother somehow stopped his sense from working and gave him a look of a parent in control.

'But, Bramble, what's to happen to her when we go to the gathering, Grandma? Can she come too?'

His grandma just nodded towards the dog, and Dill realised she was gnawing away on a big bone. This meant that she would be occupied for the next couple of hours. When she had a bone, she was completely focused on the job in hand – a doggy ninja in full concentration.

It was time to go, and Dill watched his grandma pulling on long green Wellington boots. She made him wear his too, because she said that there were lots of boggy bits in the wood. He realized that the walk would be squidgy and mucky, which was probably why the dog couldn't come with them.

Outside there were flocks of starlings flying in the sky, creating a great spectacle as hundreds of them flew in one direction and then without warning shot off in another, making a beautiful picture of changing patterns that reminded him of the kaleidoscope he'd got for Christmas two years before. Hares and rabbits were bouncing all over the ground and the sounds of all the creatures moving at the same time and calling out to each other as they went was like nothing he'd ever heard before. Excitement was in the air.

Grandma headed off at her best pace and he tried to keep up with her with little hops and skips around the puddles and mud patches.

'Grandma, where are the Brabbits? Aren't they coming with us?'

She answered him in sense with a picture of the Brabbit family sitting together in the centre of a wooded area by a big flat stone that was partly covered by white and green mossy stuff. He quite literally got the picture, so he didn't ask any more questions, just tried his best to keep up with the very robust older woman as she thrust her way through the long wet grassy area at the back of the standing stones and headed to the sloping hills at the foot of the old wood.

This was as far as Dill had been allowed to come before, but now he found himself walking up the hillside. Small slim silver trees were scattered over it, which his grandma was grabbing onto to pull herself higher up the incline. It was steeper than it first appeared.

As they got further up the slope, the trees became taller and the wood became denser, until they reached what appeared to be the top and Grandma stopped for a breather. A couple of deep breaths later, she looked at Dill and he instinctively knew she was ready to head deeper into the wood. In keeping with the rest of the dells countryside, it first went up and then there was a drop, and all sorts of creatures were heading that way.

There was so much to try and take in. Dill's sense was quite good now, but he was surrounded by animals and birds, and didn't have the capacity to receive all the messages of sight, sound and feeling at the same time, not to mention keep an eye on what was in front of him, so he let it all blend into a hum around him.

He only had a moment to notice the big red sun in the sky, almost directly above the centre of the old wood; its light was soft, tranquil. In that instant he thought he could see a golden layer of thin cloud building around the tops of the silver birch trees, but his grandma's urgency pulled him back on course and he had to watch his step. They both had to dig their heels into the soft marshy ground that ran on a downward slope towards the centre of the wooded area. Now they were using the trees to slow themselves down as the decline was becoming steeper.

Grandma stopped for a second and held on to a small oak tree. Dill noticed her looking up at the higher branches, where a dark greyish-brown owl with long feathery ears was perched.

In sense she said, 'Evening, Alice. Have you read my memories?'

The owl responded by nodding her head slowly, then lifting it again and winking her left eye at Grandma.

The gesture seemed to please the old lady, as she smiled and carried on heading down into the tree-filled gorge.

For a fleeting second Dill caught some of the words around him. 'She's got a nerve coming here,' a lady swan was whispering to a mallard duck.

'I've heard she's nice and full of sense,' an old male otter was saying to a female badger who Dill could have sworn was called Wilma. 'She's supposed to have lived here many, many goddesses ago.'

There was so much going on it was hard to stay focused on any one thing at a time. Three frogs seemed to be in deep debate over the name 'Robert'.

'No, that can't be right,' Dill thought. He hurried on.

As they reached an opening in the woods where the ground looked flatter, they saw an amazing sight: animals and birds of every description for as far the eye could see. At first glance it was difficult to pick out any one creature, but the big heron that came to the bog at the back of Moon Cottage seemed to stand out for a second as he stretched his head up over the mass of smaller animals that were squished together and made a 'hrm, hrm' kind of sound as if he was looking to get someone's attention.

Dill had been instructed to stick to sense at the gathering and not use human words. His grandma told him that words might startle the other creatures and one of the reasons she'd got him in was because he could use the language of the dells creatures.

They were walking very slowly now, taking care where they put their feet, as there were so many small creatures like mice, voles, frogs and toads all over the floor of the clearing. But the more the animals noticed the humans walking among them, the more a path opened in front of them, and much of the sound of sense dropped to no more than a slight hum which in any language would have sounded like a long drawn out 'Oohhhh' sound.

'Thought she'd be taller, didn't you, Nora?'

Two squirrels were talking to each other from the trees above their head.

'Shooosh, she understands sense.'

'Says who?' Nora responded.

'Says me,' said a hooded crow that was hoping from branch to branch, trying to get to the front for a better view. 'I've met her and she has more sense than some I could mention.'

More mumblings followed, but Dill's mind was pulled ahead. He could see the stone where the Brabbits were waiting for him.

It looked exactly as it had in the picture he'd had. Jack was there, kicking out his back legs in very excited fashion, and his sisters were both fluffing themselves up to look their best for their introduction to Dill and his grandmother. Their mother was standing up on her back legs, looking anxiously in their direction.

'Now, Brabbits,' she said, 'be on your best behaviour tonight. This is very important for all of us and I don't want us to be the talk of the dells when it's over, understood?'

'Evening, Beryl. Everything OK?'

Dill shouldn't have been surprised when he heard his grandma greet Mrs Brabbit, but it always gave him a little jolt in his tummy when she used the names of the animals she met. It looked as though she knew a lot of the creatures by name and most of them knew her, or of her at least.

'Yes, thank you, Vi,' Mrs Brabbit replied. 'Just leave Dill with us, he'll be fine. And remember, Vi, I'll be sending you all my light. Just keep your mind clear – it all comes back, dear.'

Grandma thanked her and headed off in the direction of the first bunch of animals they'd seen on entering the clearing, including the long-eared owl called Alice and the tall heron.

Jack was so excited to see Dill, and both Bunty and Droopsy were thrilled to meet him, though almost too shy to speak. Mrs Brabbit behaved just like any adult would when looking after a group of children at a large event and began to give out instructions about sticking together and not wandering off and being on their best behaviour in front of the Lord of the Dells and all the other creatures. Then she suddenly realised that in all the excitement she hadn't even welcomed Dill properly.

'Oh, Dillan, I do apologise. Where are my manners? Please sit on the stone beside us and may I say it is a pleasure to have you in our little family for this evening.'

Dill politely thanked the lady rabbit and squeezed into the small space between Jack and his sisters. He was wondering why his grandma had left him and gone off in the other direction when his friend said, 'Look up, mate, quick.'

Dill suddenly noticed that all the creatures were stretching their necks skywards, and then, as he tilted his head back, he could see why.

The sun was dropping behind the old wood, but a big silver moon was now in the sky, moving up to the top of the hill of the fairies to the east of where they were sitting. It looked as if it was about to touch the top of the wish tree.

As the fading red sun poured the last of its rays into the little amphitheatre at the centre of the old wood, the floor of the clearing blazed with an iridescent yellow, which seemed to reflect back from the ground into the sky above them, making the circle of space directly above the clearing a brilliant amber colour. As Dill gazed upwards, it became alive with little fairy lights sparkling white in the amber glow, and just for a moment he thought that there were tiny people inside them.

There was complete hush for a moment. The sound of sense was replaced by the sound of silence as the atmosphere became thin and a light golden cloud cut across the sun. There was a sharp intake of breath as it took the form of the young goddess of spring. She appeared to be wearing a long yellow gown and a crown of leaves and flowers. The light that came from her was gold and white, and a soft warm breeze blew over the gathering as she let out a short breath. 'Aaahhh...' Her eyes twinkled with what could only be described as a joyful mischief, which ran through every creature simultaneously, including Dill.

As the 'Aaahhh...' left her lips again, they knew that Brigisha's reign had truly begun.

In that magical moment the creatures of the dells were so hypnotised by the goddess's appearance that no one noticed that the great white stag had taken his place in the centre of the arena. Then he raised his head to the sky and spoke.

'Let the justice of the great mother of all nature prevail.'

Dill's jaw dropped. The light around the magnificent animal filled the empty space with sparkling white and gold dust particles, and the feeling of lightness was almost too much to bear. He felt his head swimming for a brief moment.

In an instant there were hundreds of visions in the space around the great stag, memories of past offences committed by all the different predators of the dip 'n' dells, flashes of eagles and owls and weasels and stoats, wildcats and foxes and some Dill had neither seen nor heard of before. It appeared that in that second thousands of cases were settled, because on elevated levels of sense like this gathering, there are no limitations or complications, and of course you can't lie when you are in the presence of one with as much sense as the great white stag.

The tiny white lights shot hither and thither, giving and taking, appearing and disappearing in and out of space and time. Their job was to present memories of what was true, so help them, goddess.

Mrs Brabbit was happy, because it was deemed that her case was settled without complication. Jonnie Fox had taken her husband out of hunger, so he received his pardon with her grace, because it was part of nature's law and all creatures had to abide by that. The fact that she already knew that Mr Brabbit was in Light Land helped her to accept that his hard body had been used to help another creature survive. She knew that the real part of him, his light, was safe and watching over her and their family from above.

Dill was shocked at how soon the court session was over. He found it hard to take in, but was still totally caught up in the buzz of the moment, the little light beings, the joy that was being created and the happiness that everyone was experiencing. And Jack was sitting on his lap now and both his sisters were snuggling into his side, and all were in a state of bliss because their mother was happy and life could truly move on.

The court cases weren't all about predators. The three frogs Dill had heard on entering the gathering were having a dispute over which one should own the name 'Robert', but Dill didn't find out which one got it in the end, as all he heard of that case was 'Robert, Robert, and Robert.'

He also caught a bit of a case about a pair of skylarks, Mr and Mrs Shrill, who couldn't have chicks. Somehow it was deemed that not every couple could have children; sometimes nature did this to show people that not even love could control nature, but Mr and Mrs Shrill were given the promise of hope for next spring.

Dill could hear these cases only because they were conducted near to where he was sitting, but sense told him that there were still others that were so complicated that the whole gathering had to witness them, and they were referred to as 'clearances'. The older, more sense-filled animals would deal with them much as a judge and jury would. As he wondered what that would be like, he forgot that his thoughts were like words to the animals around him.

'Shush,' Mrs Brabbit said, as she could hear his contemplation getting louder. 'There is to be a clearance now and I want you all to listen in.'

Dill was excited, but nervous at the same time. He was sure that he could feel nervousness coming from Jack's mother too. Why was that?

Then everything became clear in an instant when he heard the Lord of the Dells announce: 'Let me call the accused: Mrs Violet Thornberry of Moon Cottage.'

'Grandma!'

Dill knew he wasn't to speak, but he couldn't stop himself from calling out as he watched his grandmother being led slowly forward.

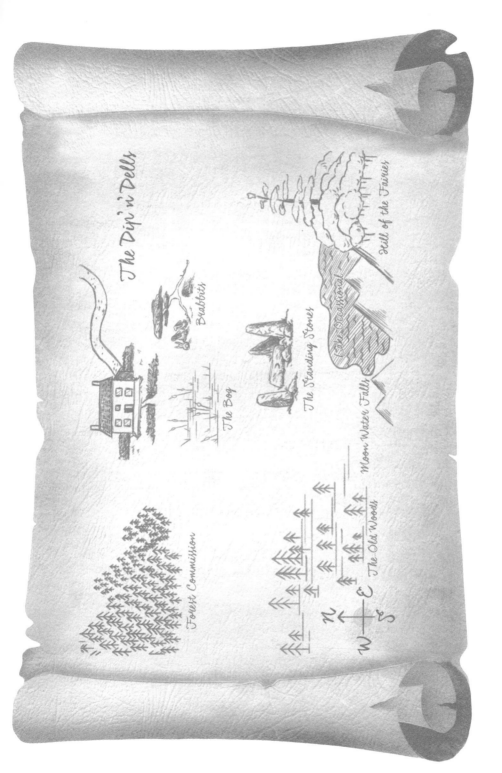

The Dip'n'Dells

Brabbith

Forest Commission

The Bog

The Standing Stones

Moon Water Falls

The Old Woods

Hill of the Fairies

The Occasional Lake

N
W E
S

Chapter Nine
Clearance and Understanding

'Silence!' was the call that went up from the great stag.

In her best sense voice, Mrs Brabbit turned to Dill and told him that he must not use human words or he would be removed from the gathering. In silence he gazed at his grandma as she stood before the Lord of the Dells, looking small and alone.

'You are Mrs Violet Thornberry of Moon Cottage,' he said in a deep commanding tone that was felt by all the onlookers. 'You are known to some as "the woman of the dells".'

'That is correct, my lord,' she responded, straightening herself up to look him directly in the eye.

All around the arena Dill could feel that the creatures were impressed by her command of the sense language. Mutterings began to leak out and a magpie called out, 'Give 'er a fair trial, you lot. I know what it's like to be persecuted for my own nature.'

'Don't listen to him, he's a thief and a liar!' a whole family of blue tits called in response.

Suddenly comments were ringing out around the open arena. Beaks were raised, wings aflutter, tails flapping like nobody's business. It was bedlam and again the stag called for hush.

He addressed Dill's grandmother once more.

'You understand why you have been called to the predators' pardon under the guidance of the goddess Brigisha?'

'Yes, I do, my lord, and I intend to claim my right to be here in the dells and clear my name of the charge levelled against me tonight. I would like to make it known that I am a peace-loving dells creature and show that I am in no way and have never been at any time a predator or any threat to a single creature of the dip 'n' dells, or for that matter any other place.'

'And are you represented here today, Mrs Thornberry?'

'Yes, my lord. My counsel is Alice Otus of the old wood.'

Oohs and aahs went around the gathering, as Alice Otus was known to be a formidable speaker of sense who had lived for many goddesses and was very well versed in the laws of Mother Nature.

'She's fabulous,' a mother pheasant told her 12 children. 'She's fought many cases, but she only does so when she feels that her defendant is in the right. Many of her results have led to new understandings here.'

'Yes,' Mrs Brabbit said. 'That's why Grandma left you here with us, Dillan – she had to have someone to defend her, and Alice Otus is the very best.'

Light grew around Dill and the Brabbit family, and others could see it.

'Many creatures are complaining about the humans in the dells again,' Mrs Brabbit explained, 'and almost none, except a few that your grandma has conversed with, believe that she is tame and non-threatening. But don't worry, she is in good wings with old Alice.'

As she spoke, Alice Otus swooped down from the small oak and landed on a tree root which stuck out from the boggy ground in front of the great stag. She bowed her head to him, then turned towards three boulders on her left, which were occupied by the truth-tellers, who were like the jury in a human court.

Alice clasped her wings behind her back and bowed to them, then looked directly at them with her big round yellow eyes and winked the left one in the same way as when greeting Dill's grandma.

'My lords and lady.'

Her opponent today would be the tall grey heron, who was named Ardea Spears, though he was more commonly known to the creatures as the patient assassin.

Dill wanted to know how he got his name, and Jack hurriedly told him, 'It's because he waits so long in one place to catch his prey. He is said to be the most patient deliberator in the dells.'

Many of the creatures nodded in anticipation when his name was called, as they could foresee a good battle of wits between these two equally talented masters of sense.

The heron took his time before bowing his long neck to the truth-tellers.

'My lords and lady.'

'What's going to happen?' Dill asked Mrs Brabbit in his best sense voice.

She explained quickly that in a clearance the prosecutor would present the charges to the truth-tellers, who would then call the council for the defence to reply, and then the verdict would be reached by the truth-tellers, sometimes in seconds.

In this case the central truth-teller was a golden eagle named Aquila. She sat on the middle boulder. She was considered wise because she was the highest flyer in the dells and had a better perspective on things than even the buzzards.

To the right of Aquila sat an old badger, Berty, who had been a successful defence council for many years and now in his old age had been called to the high seats as a truth-teller.

The last of the three, sitting to the left of the impressive eagle, was Norbu, the oldest of all the hares in the dells. In his day he had been a great boxing champion. He had never lost a contest in the space of 12 goddesses, which had gained him the reputation having more awareness and cunning than any other hare in the land.

The heron, Ardea, now opened the case for the prosecution.

'Violet Thornberry appears to be a nice person,' he told the three truth-tellers, 'but is she? She speaks sense – we have witnessed this, as have some of the gathering – and that is one reason why we are here this evening. We are here to decide whether or not we can trust this woman and her brood. We are here to challenge her claim that she is "gentle and peace-loving", as she puts it, and we will prove to you all something other than what you have been told and what you see. Then we will let sense prevail.'

He nodded his long-pointed bill towards the judges and then the stag, and turned to Alice, who had both eyes closed as if she was concentrating deeply.

'Now,' he said. 'I call Mrs Violet Thornberry to the stag.'

This meant that Grandma would have to put her hand on the chest of the Lord of the Dells and allow him access to some of her memories. She was happy to do this, as she and Alice had discussed it earlier. She really wanted all of the creatures to see her childhood in their land and feel the love she had for it and know that the creatures in her day had accepted her and her grandmother.

'My lord, you may search my mind to the time of my childhood and reveal it to the gathering,' she said. 'I have no objections. Please do this until you are satisfied that neither I nor my family will threaten you or any other creature of this place.'

The gathering was silent with anticipation. This was taking the trial to another level: all the creatures would be given access to the memories and feelings of a human being.

The stag closed his thinking mind and opened his heart, and a pure white light formed a screen-like bubble around him and began to transmit images in all directions of Violet Thornberry's early life in the dip 'n' dells.

Dill, like every other member of the gathering, was flabbergasted by what he saw: his grandmother as a girl, playing, talking to and loving animals, insects, flowers, trees and little light people like the ones he had seen earlier. The scenes washed over the gathering like the wind and came to an end, like the earlier trials, in an instant.

'Wow!' The air was filled with wonderment and all of the creatures simultaneously extended their light towards Violet Thornberry. She removed her hand from the chest of the stag and gave a polite bow of acceptance around the arena.

Dill was stuck for words, even in sense. Light and love were being extended to his grandma from around the gathering. But beneath the rapturous reception a certain sound was growing in volume: 'Hrm, hrm, hrm.'

Ardea Spears was patiently standing on one leg, head lifted halfway between full length and shoulders. Eventually all the creatures turned their attention towards him. Dill could feel a sort of grounding begin to enter his body.

'My lords and lady, if I may bring the attention of the gathering back to good sense and address the other matter of why the lady is standing stag-side at the moment.'

Everyone gathered now had the feeling that Dill had, and it felt as though a large stone had dropped into a mud splat.

'Is it not true, Mrs Thornberry, that in the early part of the guardianship of the goddess Cailasha you came across a white goose beside Lake Occasional? The bird was not a resident of the dells but was stopping for a rest midway through its long journey west.'

The heron raised his long neck from between his shoulders and the power in his delivery was ferocious.

'Is it not true that you captured the bird and took it to your dwelling, after which you left the dwelling with the bird under a cover of sorts and bundled it into the machine that gave smoke from its rear and the poor bird was never seen again? I put it to the truth-tellers that this woman of the dells killed that bird, and not out of hunger either.'

Outraged squealing and howling came from all quarters of the amphitheatre.

'Silence!' said the stag. 'There will be order at this meeting. May I remind you all that you are still in the presence of a goddess.'

Silence fell at once.

Ardea's long neck was still stretched to its fullest, his head moving sharply from one area of the arena to another. He made sure he looked round all the creatures before drawing his neck down so that it was hunched between his shoulders, then concluded with a nod to the judges.

Alice, however, was ready for this – in fact she had prepared for just such an outburst. Grandma had sensed this would be brought up and it was why she needed Alice's defence.

Alice stretched her neck, wobbled her head and rolled her shoulders back three times before lifting her right wing to point towards Dill's grandmother.

'This lady did come across a white goose by the lake in Cailasha's time, and yes, she did take it to her home, and yes, Ardea, you were correct to report to the gathering that she drove it away in her motor car.'

She then took a moment to explain to the gathering in a very superior, almost smug manner that this was what the humans called the machine in question.

Much nodding and soft mumbling followed this statement, as many of the creatures tried to understand the pictures of a car that came from the sense the owl projected.

'But she didn't take the bird away to kill it,' Alice continued. 'No, she took it to a human who saves the lives of creatures. Violet Thornberry isn't a killer – she was trying to save the exhausted bird's life out of care and compassion, the same care and compassion you have witnessed for yourselves and that she has displayed in the dells for more goddesses than any of you can imagine. I put it to you that this good woman of Moon Cottage is no more a predator than little Jack Brabbit.'

Jack's eyes widened at the mention of his name at such a prestigious event.

'Cool, Jack,' Dill whispered to his friend.

The little rabbit fluffed up. 'Aw thanks, Dill.'

A buzz was now going round the gathering. Dill was wondering if Alice had given a good enough speech to convince the judges when he felt Mrs Brabbit send him a sense message that it wasn't finished.

'What will happen next?' he thought, as he watched Alice Otus roll her eyes round to look directly at the truth-tellers.

Most of the creatures were feeling it was a very close call at this point, and within a second they got confirmation that the judges felt the same. Instead of giving their verdict quickly, they asked the heron if he would like to carry on.

Standing on one leg, which was as yellow as Alice's eyes, he nodded and half-extended his neck once more.

'One thing only remains to be said,' he commented.

He began to walk deliberately over the muddy ground with his wings clasped behind his back, then lifted his eyes to look around the arena once more.

Slowly and deliberately, he asked, 'Did the bird live, Mrs Thornberry?'

Instantly loud cries came from all sides. So passionate were the calls from the crowd that the great stag lifted his front leg and banged his hoof on the ground.

His message was felt in an instant and once again there was order.

The stag looked expectantly at Alice, who was fluffing out her feathers and straightening the two long ear-like feathers on the top of her head. She looked directly back at him before replying.

'The answer,' she said, with a slight break in her voice, 'is that the bird died at the hands of the man Violet took it to in order to save its life.'

A tremor went through the gathering, but the creatures knew not to defy the stag again, so they remained silent. The outrage they all felt was expressed instead in a feeling of coldness that swept through the gathering. Even the light began to fade.

Dill was very worried for his grandma now, and not so confident in Alice either. He wondered how he hadn't seen his grandma bringing a great big white goose into the cottage – but maybe it had happened on one of the days when he was with Jack and Grandma was out for hours with Bramble.

Alice Otus ruffled her feathers and pulled herself up as tall as possible before she spoke again.

'I would like to ask my lord if he would permit Mrs Thornberry to share her memories of that day with the gathering. I feel, my lord, that it is the only way that we will make sense of what really happened on that unfortunate day and I'm certain it will exonerate the lady in question.'

There was a moment's consideration from the stag, but then he looked straight at the wise owl and nodded his head in agreement.

Grandma had already asked Alice if she could present these memories to the gathering, but her counsel hadn't thought it would be necessary to do so. The owl had felt the stag would allow a clearance after the childhood memories had been shared, but the heron had put up a stronger case than she had imagined.

'Let it be remembered,' said the stag, 'that in the language of sense only our true thoughts, feelings and memories can be displayed, so there is no way that what you are about to see could be false. Violet Thornberry, step forward once more.'

The old lady did as requested, once again placed her right hand on the great stag's heart and began to recall the day she'd found the white goose. The light around the stag began to brighten and expand in all directions and once more a series of pictures began to build.

The first picture showed Mrs Thornberry walking by the side of the lake with the big dog called Bramble. She appeared to be teaching her sense with the help of Mrs Brabbit in order to introduce her to the Brabbit family. All the creatures felt at once that her reason for doing this was to show the dog ways not to harm little animals. There was a feeling of softness in this picture that made all the animals connect in light.

The next picture was of a white goose lying on its side by a rock at the side of the shallow Lake Occasional and calling out in pain. The creatures all watched Grandma walk towards the bird while making the dog stay behind so as not to alarm the bird any more. She then asked the goose in sense if she could try to help her and the goose agreed, but felt that her end was near as her neck was broken. She thanked the woman for her kindness. Then, as the heron had said, Grandma picked up the bird and did everything else he had mentioned in the trial.

The next set of memories came from a place which no animal at the gathering had ever seen before. Two humans, a male and female, and Grandma were standing around the bird, who was now lying on a large table, and the humans were trying to fix her. All the animals at the gathering felt the love that was being given to the goose, and some were even crying because they hadn't known anything like that could happen in the human world.

The other thing that was felt was the pain that the goose was feeling. In sense, an animal can feel another's pain, and at that moment the entire collection of animals observing the scene felt the pain of the badly injured bird.

There followed lots of human words which translated into compassion and healing, and the creatures watched the male human stick something into the bird's body as Grandma sent it her light. The pain slowly ended and the light body separated and began to ascend into Light Land.

The final picture was one of a single tear running down the old lady's cheek as a soft smile broke across her face.

Many of the creatures were holding back tears themselves now, including Dill and all of the Brabbit family. A great sigh went around the gathering as the scene ended.

Grandma stepped back from the great stag and bowed her head.

Much of the earlier brightness of the gathering had gone now and there was just a pale pink light in the sky to show where the setting sun had disappeared behind the old wood.

The tall heron closed his eyes and fell silent.

Alice was the first of the court creatures to speak. She waddled along her root and said in a very clear voice: 'I feel, my lord and truth-tellers, that this action shows us several things. I feel that it shows bravery on the part of Violet Thornberry and I feel that it shows compassion as well as her love for animals in that she ended the suffering of a creature who was in real pain and whose life was ending anyway. What this lady did was what any bird does when she recognises that an egg in her nest will not give life and evicts it. Or, for that matter, what any mother fox does when she recognises that a newborn cub is lame or suffering and ends its life for the good of the healthy cubs in the litter. My lord, only someone with true sense could perform such an act and I say that Violet Thornberry of Moon Cottage is such a lady.'

She swivelled her head in all directions, ending with a long look at the truth-tellers, and the wink of her left eye told them that her speech had ended.

There was a short exchange between the truth-tellers, and then the stag lifted his large head and addressed the gathering once more.

'The goddess has heard this case, as have the truth-tellers and I,' he said in a much softer tone than when he had opened the gathering. 'It has been left to me, though, to come to a verdict and decide upon the fate of Violet Thornberry. This is what I feel.'

He brought new understanding to all the creatures when he told them that he had just learned, as they had, that there seemed to be a difference between taking the life of another being and ending its suffering. In this case he felt that Mrs Thornberry was responsible for ending the suffering of the goose and had therefore acted out of compassion. He advised all the creatures to learn from this, though he added that not all humans behaved in that manner and the dells creatures must still be wary of them. However, Mrs Thornberry and her grandson, Dill, would not ever be seen as predators in the land of the dip 'n' dells.

He concluded by thanking Grandma for acting so swiftly, for showing consideration of the pain and suffering of the goose and for understanding the value of sending light to a dying creature, as it would indeed have assisted the light body of the bird into Light Land. He closed his speech by saying that although in nature it was not right to end the life of another being without just cause, bringing the pain of the goose to an end was a just cause.

Light rose in every creature simultaneously and the gathering was ablaze with colour and joy. The goddess Brigisha smiled down on them and swished across the sky playfully before disappearing behind the old wood, chasing the sun to wherever it went. The great stag disappeared too and the dip 'n' dells was left with a feeling of balance and harmony.

It was a thin place and a thin time, which meant that beauty could be born from pain, and from endings there would be new beginnings. It was also the time to look beyond old thoughts and feelings and see life from a higher perspective. Brigisha was telling the entire living world to look to her for hope and joy and the strength to begin again.

Chapter Ten
The Moods of Spring

The first weeks that followed the spring gathering were as tempestuous as the teenage-like goddess herself; for the first two weeks of her stay, there were four seasons every day. Showers of rain came pouring out of the sky like great waterfalls, and the winds that moved the rain on were so strong they made the water look as though it was bending sideways as they escorted it away in a south-easterly direction. Sometimes the sky would be bright and clear with sunshine, yet at other times snow would fall, only to disappear before reaching the now beautifully coloured floor of the dip 'n' dells. Flowers of all description had burst open, and every new day of Brigisha's reign brought more buds popping out of the ground and blossom decorating the trees.

'Brigisha brings everything above the surface in her season; she is unashamedly honest and wants nothing to be hidden. She reveals all that is beautiful and new, but she also teaches us about the challenges that lie ahead. Even the most perfect flower will have to withstand the harsh winds and changeable conditions that come in the first part of her season. Every creature knows that this is one of the most important times for survival. But those who endure the hardships of early spring will be stronger for it, and for them there is always the promise of a long fruitful summer.'

Grandma was telling Dill, Jack and his two sisters all about the goddess of spring under a piece of flat board held up by two posts with a big green tarpaulin slung over it: Dill's den. She had had the great idea of building a little lean-to that would cover the tunnel that led to the Brabbits' place, and it had been made from materials that had come from the shed when Dill's parents had cleared it out. Now Dill could spend time with his friends in a place that was safe for the little rabbits. It had become a daily meeting-place.

'You have to wonder if the goddesses are in fact different women or just different stages of womanhood that display every side of feminine wisdom and the compassion of Mother Nature herself,' Grandma went on. 'Brigisha seems to show us all the transformational and yet turbulent energy that youth brings. She has an abundance of life-changing power and aspirations for new things. She is youthful, she can afford to give, and there is no greater gift a young female can give to this world than her true self and her willingness to bring new life.'

'Grandma Vi,' Flopsy Brabbit asked, lifted her ears up, 'does the goddess Brigisha never grow old?'

'Well, sweetheart, none of us really grow old inside, we just change like the seasons.'

Grandma would have loved to have answered more questions for the youngsters, but she knew it was time to move on, because Bramble, who was keeping watch in the garden, was making noises and sensing that Dill's parents were around.

'Come now, children.' Mrs Brabbit, that vehicle of sense, had poked her head through the hole in the wall. 'We need to get on with things. There is so much to do and Grandma Vi has much to attend to herself.'

It was true. Grandma had to go back to her other house to sort out some overdue affairs. She would be gone for two weeks. That was another reason for building the den. She knew that Dill's parents wouldn't let him go out alone for walks but would have no problem with him spending time in the garden, and that way he could keep up his friendship with the Brabbits.

There had been much talking in the den about Grandma's trial, which had really brought them all much closer together. All of the Brabbit children were now addressing her as 'Grandma Vi', which she loved. In fact, many of the animals in the dells were calling her this and it seemed that since the night of Brigisha's arrival there was much more respect for her and for Dill himself. He noticed that when they walked together many of the creatures would move closer to them than they had ever dared to before.

On a couple of evenings Dill had watched from his bedroom window as Alice Otus had flown into the garden to talk sense with his grandma, though he had never been able to pick up on their conversations. It made him wonder if his grandma had the same kind of friendship with the wise old owl as he had with Jack. He was certain grandma had been very close to Rowena, her childhood friend, and to others she talked about from that time, like Gloria the swan and an otter named Flo. Her adventures back then sounded amazing and he wondered if he would get to have some great new adventures of his own – as if talking to animals wasn't exciting enough!

So often when he was getting ready for bed now he would hear his parents having an argument downstairs. It always seemed as if they waited until he'd gone to his room before lashing out at each other.

'If only I couldn't hear it,' he thought.

'Is it my fault, Tom? Am I the one who doesn't want to talk anymore?'

There was a low mumbling sound, which he knew to be his father responding quietly, as if quiet arguing was better.

Dill turned his attention away from the human world again and at once he could hear his grandma talking to Mrs Brabbit in the garden.

'So, you've got everything packed and ready then, Violet?'

'Yes, I won't be gone too long. I just need to tie up all the loose ends of my old life and then I'll be back. Oh, and thank you, Beryl, I know he is in good hands.'

'Well, I will do what I can, and as long as the children have each other their minds will be occupied.'

'Yes, and Dill being in the garden will keep his parents out of the dells, which will be a good thing.'

'Why's that?' Dill thought vaguely.

He was under the covers now and Bramble was lying beside him. She had already said goodnight to him and was now snoring, which was comforting in a way because it became the predominant noise in the house.

'It's strange,' Dill thought, 'how Bramble only really uses sense in the open air.'

It seemed that it was difficult for her to do so indoors somehow. She was always just his dog in the house, and in some ways that was nice; it was normal and it made him relax.

He tried for a moment to hear his grandma and Mrs Brabbit again, but they must have sensed him listening and blocked him out. This was something the older sense beings were doing more often, he thought.

As he lay awake in his bed that night, he thought about what his grandma had said about the strong winds bending the little flowers in spring. Had Amber been one of those that just didn't make it through the season? So often lately, he took his grandma's words to bed with him.

But even in the turbulent weather of early spring he was quite happy and settled in the dip 'n' dells. He knew that he would make it through. He had new friends and the most amazing adventures ahead of him. Somehow he knew that the best was yet to come.

He woke late the following morning to find that his grandma had already left. She must have gone at the crack of dawn, because his father was already back from dropping her at the train station at Upper Dell, and that was 20 miles away.

The kitchen was quiet and both his parents were reading newspapers that his father had picked up from the little newsstand by the station. Dill had never been to the train station, but his grandma had told him about all the places around the dells, especially the village of Upper Dell, which was where she used to cycle to when she wanted to buy things.

On the evening of the spring gathering Dill had hoped that his parents would come back from the town happier. They'd had their dinner at the restaurant as planned and had even spent the night in the only hotel in the town. But since their return his mother had become even quieter than before and when his father hadn't been in his office he'd been busying himself with trips in and out of town. In fact, when Dill thought about it, he realised his parents never really sat down and talked to each other these days. The only time he ever heard them converse was during the arguments after he'd gone to bed.

'It's so difficult to understand grown-ups,' he thought. 'They teach you about truth and honesty and then they keep things hidden, either from you or from other adults.'

Even the adult sense beings had a way of blocking sense from the young ones, he knew, but somehow that did feel different. He didn't know why, but it didn't seem so hidden or hurtful.

He felt kind of angry with his parents today for some reason. Maybe it was because his grandma had left, or because they never seemed to fix what was happening to them. He felt that they were very selfish – or was he being selfish?

He sighed. Every time he got cross with his parents, he felt guilty about it. And sad too. Why couldn't they be happy, or even normal, like he was? Maybe that was wrong too, though, maybe he shouldn't feel normal or happy. His sister had died, after all.

His thinking was dull today. It seemed so hard to lift his thoughts. Even thinking was hard; it was much easier to just observe.

His mother, who was sitting opposite him, wasn't biting her nails today, he noticed. But that was because she had run out of nail and was now chewing the skin on the nail-bed.

He gave another sigh and Bramble came by and sat at his side. His hand automatically dropped onto her head and he felt his mood lighten a little.

He looked in his father's direction and saw him sitting reading his paper, legs crossed, with his right leg constantly rocking up and down over his left. The tension in the room was mounting by the second.

Suddenly his father looked up from his paper and spoke.

'Dill, your mother and I are going to let you take us out into the countryside today so that you can show us some of the things you've learned from all those walks you've had with Grandma.'

What? Dill was stunned. His parents never wanted to do anything together nowadays, let alone go for walks in the wild countryside! The last time his mother had gone out to the dells she'd run back in after standing on the stones. Since then she'd never even looked over the garden wall. And as for his father, he'd never been keen on nature in his life.

What, Dill wondered, could he possibly show them that would be of interest to them?

His mother smiled at him and added, 'Yes, we need to spend more time with you and we know that you've been learning about all the wildlife here, so we thought we'd take a picnic lunch out. What do you say?'

He didn't say anything, but excitement was already replacing the glum heavy feeling inside him.

Bramble meanwhile had been in full swing ever since his father had said the word 'out'. The dog was doing what his father called 'the springer shuffle' – a dance where her front paws bounced up and down and her back end swung from side to side.

Dill could hear her sense reaction; it was singing: 'Oh my, oh my, oh my, I'm going out to the countryside – I'm going out to be totally wild!'

'Ha, ha, ha, ha!' His father's deep laugh was a comfort, a real treat to hear, and Dill could never contain himself when the dog went crazy; he was on his feet dancing with her.

'Steady on, everyone, I've got some dishes to wash, and you need to wear country clothes for walking out here, mister.'

His mother spoke with some authority, but smiled a genuine smile at her husband as she flicked a dishcloth in his direction.

Dill could see that his parents were genuinely making an effort.

'Somebody please let that dog out of this house or we will all be infected by her madness!'

His mother was half-laughing now and doing a little dance too, which made Dill laugh as he shuffled to the back door and released the brown and white flash to freedom.

As he dashed upstairs and threw on his clothes, he could hear his father singing in his bedroom downstairs. For once he sounded really happy. Dill couldn't help thinking how amazing this all was. But he couldn't think for long – it was time to hurry up and join Bramble outside.

Five minutes later, Dill and his mother were waiting by the back door when Dill saw the strangest sight coming their way: a man in camouflage trousers and jacket with a small cap of the same cloth on his head, binoculars around his neck and a large staff in his hand with a small antler as a handle. He looked just like a commando. Even the boots he was wearing made him look as though he was going off to war.

'Now this is what a real hunter looks like, Rose.'

Dill laughed inside, but said nothing. He had never seen his father look like this, and he felt a bit sorry for him.

His mother took absolutely no notice of her husband's camouflage gear, but headed for the coat rack to grab her jacket. It was the jacket she always wore nowadays, Dill thought. She always wore the same jeans and jumper as well. On reflection, it had been ages since she'd worn any of the nice clothes she used to wear in the old house. Even her hair looked like Brigisha's did – all wild and frizzy and unkempt. He felt sorry for her too. She didn't seem to care what she looked like these days. Well, neither did his father, obviously.

As they left through the back door of the cottage Dill spoke sense to Bramble and asked her to nip round to the front of the Brabbits' burrow and tell them that he was going out walking with his parents so that they wouldn't be worried about him.

No sooner had the dog received the message than she was over the wall.

'I'm on it,' she called out as she went.

'Bramble, come back here, girl,' his father called.

'She's fine, Dad,' Dill reassured him, 'she knows every inch of the place already, even more than Grandma, and that's a lot. She'll catch us up by the old wood up there.'

Dill figured that was the best place to take his parents. He knew the way there and he also knew that they might see some of the wild creatures of the dells there. From the hilltop at the edge of the wood they would get great views of the hill of the fairies, and they would even see a bit of Lake Occasional, which was still quite swollen.

Suddenly he wondered whether some of the animals would come close to him and want to hear him talking sense, the way they did when he was with his grandma. What should he do? But no sooner was the thought out of his mind than he heard, 'I'm on it.'

Bramble shot past, giving the little high-pitched barking sounds that his parents thought were cute, but he heard as 'Keep your distance, guys – the two older humans have no sense.'

Dill chuckled to himself. The dog was sending her message out on the breeze. This was a sort of social network in the dells where creatures could send sense out on the air for all within reach to hear.

'Ah, shut up, crazy dog, you're scaring things away.' A kestrel who was hunting for food, wasn't best pleased to hear Bramble.

A couple of old field mice had different ideas, though. 'Cheers for that, Bramble,' they called from the long grass.

To Dill, the air was loud with conversation; to his parents' untrained sense, it was just the buzz and hum of the countryside they lived in.

They wandered past the standing stones, and Dill was very aware that his mother couldn't look at them; she kept her head down and looked at the ground as they walked past. His sense told him that they frightened her and he remembered how abruptly she'd left him on their visit there in the autumn. He wondered why she would be afraid of some big stones, but was distracted by his father whispering loudly, 'Shush, everyone stop! Now don't move, but there is a young deer at the edge of the wood. Oh my God, he's just standing there. Can you believe it?'

He held out his arm and tried to get everyone in line behind him, as if they were in some sort of covert operation.

'I think he knows we're here, Tom.'

'Shush! Don't say a word or you'll frighten him.'

Dill was giggling but trying to muffle the sound with his hand. He knew that the deer already knew they were there and that 'he' was actually a 'she' called Gisela. He had met her many times on his travels with his grandma.

'Sorry, Gisela, they're parents – they don't have any sense.'

For Dill it was like friends of his age being introduced to his out-of-touch dad – a bit embarrassing, to say the least. But the deer wasn't offended; she was as interested in them as they were in her.

'No worries, Dill, but I'm gonna disappear when they blink, if that's OK?'

Dill told her it was and thanked her for letting them see her.

His mother was quite calm about the whole thing. She'd seen animals in the wild in her childhood, but his father was blown away by it. He was a city man after all, and loved the whole stalking thing. He crouched down and lifted his binoculars gingerly.

'Dad, please don't do that. She knows that you're there and if you act like you're stalking her she'll know and run off. Just be natural, eh?'

Dill's father was quite put out, but he knew his son was right because the deer had disappeared before he'd even got his binoculars to his face.

Dill tried to ease things by telling his parents that animals were as curious about humans as humans were about them.

'If they knew that we meant them no harm, they'd let us see them,' he said. 'They'd be watching us!'

His mother gave a little laugh and he could feel that the trepidation she'd felt near the stones had gone, but he sensed that his father was still a bit put out by how things were going after all the effort he'd put into his 'natural' look.

'It's not what you look like with animals, it's what you feel like, Pops,' he said.

'Well,' his father replied, 'at least I made the effort to look as though I was going to the country to stalk wild animals. You two just look trampy.'

'What a cheek! I'll have you know it's taken me months to get this unkempt look just right,' his mother laughed. 'Fashion philistine.'

'She's almost playful now,' Dill thought. It was such a strange day.

As they reached the edge of the wood Dill couldn't help but notice how beautiful it had become since the spring gathering. The forest floor was covered with a carpet of bluebells, surrounded by glorious green grass which seemed to insulate every inch of space and create a kind of deafening silence. And above the silence, all sorts of little insects were dancing in the soft light.

'This is a perfect place to have a picnic,' Dill's mother said.

Dill could feel her body actually relaxing and he was filled with joy. His father, meanwhile, was giving off an energy that was quite childlike, something he hadn't ever noticed in him before.

'Just getting out into the dells is helping them,' he thought. 'This magic, this light, could brighten anyone.'

His parents were merrily setting about creating a lunch on a tartan blanket.

'Yes, old girl,' his father was saying, 'I do believe that you are right.'

'Hey, less of the "old girl", old boy!'

It really was the perfect place to stop. As they ate, they looked around them and they could see for miles. There was Moon Cottage, set perfectly among the small series of peaks and mounds which from this point made the land look as though it was rolling in waves towards the distant forestry plantation. And there was the hill of the fairies, with its magnificent proud wish tree, and at least a half of the lake, which was still quite an expanse of water surrounded by tall rushes and reeds.

The sun was high in the sky and the mood of young Brigisha was mellow for the first time in more than two weeks. It was the first time other than Christmas Day that Dill had felt a connection between his parents, and it made him shine from the inside.

After the picnic, he left them holding hands and talking quietly to each other and went a little way into the wood with Bramble.

'They look much better today, Bramble, don't you think?'

The dog looked up at him and gave a little sigh before answering, 'Yes, but they still need more time and many more days like this one.'

Continuing their conversation in sense, he told her, 'Yes, but I think that something that has been missing for a long time between them has come back.'

Bramble didn't answer this time; she was distracted by the shards of light that were filtering through the trees and moving across the woodland floor like searchlights. This kind of thing drove her crazy: she just had to chase the lights! Dill didn't try to force the conversation, as he knew his dog too well.

His father called over to him, 'Hey, Dill, we should do some exploring now. What do you think?'

But it was Bramble who decided where they would go for the next adventure: she tore down the hill and headed in the direction of the lake.

Lake Occasional looked massive as they approached it. From the upstairs bedrooms in the cottage they could only see a small corner of it, as the view was impeded by the hills that rose towards the hill of the fairies. Now they were able to walk all the way round it.

Dill pointed out ducks, coots, moorhens and many other birds to his father, who really didn't know what he was looking at. His mother was very impressed with his knowledge as he described how the grebes would dive under the water for food or picked out the sound of the reed buntings as they called to one another from the bullrushes.

For Dill it was a strain to keep from dropping into sense, as some of the calls he could hear around the lake were directed at him.

'Where's Grandma Vi today, Dill?' an elegant mute swan asked him as she slid by.

In order not to be rude, he had to answer quickly, 'Eh, she's gone away for a bit, but she will be back soon, I think.'

The swan glided past with the style and grace of the prima donna that she was.

'Who are the two old codgers, Dill?' an old hedgehog called out anxiously from beside a boulder. 'Hope they're not dangerous, kiddo.'

'They're not dangerous, Monty, they're my parents and I'm taking them for a walk.'

Dill had been sensing the same question from so many creatures as he'd walked through the dells that day and he was starting to feel a little weary of it. A part of him wanted to stop talking sense and just enjoy his parents' happiness for a while.

They were walking as a family, laughing and discussing how wonderful the countryside was. They *felt* like a normal family, Dill thought, like Jack's family when they all gathered round him in his den talking sense and learning about how nature worked. This had been what he'd wanted to happen and he didn't want anything to change.

As they completed the circle of the lake they approached the standing stones and Dill wondered if they should walk across the bumpy ground and avoid them. But in this new mood his mother appeared not to notice the tall circle of stones sticking out of the ground in front of her, and the little path that had been created by Grandma on her many walks there felt like the natural way to go.

'God, I really can't remember this place being so beautiful, Tom,' his mother was saying, almost oblivious to where her feet were headed. 'Mother always spoke of it as if it was wonderful, but I never got it. I suppose I was too busy studying or thinking of what dress to buy when I got home – it's like I never connected to it, you know?'

'Yeah, I never got the country at all when I was young. I played in playgrounds and parks, but that was about it. I remember my friends and I all went nuts when we saw an owl one time. It was as if we'd seen a ghost or something.'

Arm in arm, they walked on.

'God, we needed to do this for him.' Dill's father nodded in his direction.

'Yeah, I kept meaning to, but I don't know, time has just disappeared since we've been here and I think actually I didn't really want to for some reason. I was being selfish, I suppose, if I care to admit it.'

'I know exactly what you're saying. I feel the same at times, and I get caught up in so many should haves and would haves, but it's what's happening now that's really important, don't you think?'

Dill's father put his arm around his wife and pulled her closer to him as they carried on walking.

The standing stones were now up close, looking like giant hooded people standing in a circle in front of them.

Dill's father shot off towards them and jumped onto one of the small boulders that sat at the foot of the stones.

'Come on, Dill, let's climb the stones!'

Dill instinctively made for his favourite one, the one he'd been standing on when he'd first seen the goddesses in the sky, while his mother followed his father and asked to be pulled onto the same stone he was standing on.

The whole thing was great fun, and his parents' laughter and Bramble barking in her happiest sense made Dill feel even happier. But something else was happening as well. As he watched his mother leap with great dexterity onto a stone of her own, he noticed that the light was changing around her. There was something building round both his parents and he was just beginning to make it out.

Something appeared to be hanging onto his father's back, as if it was getting a piggy-back from him. It took a moment to form, but soon he could see that it was a child, only he couldn't make out who, as he was distracted by what he could see happening around his mother. She was now standing on the stone next to the one his father was on and he could see what looked like a big dark boulder inside her stomach.

Quickly he glanced back at his father, and then he realised who was holding onto him: it was Amber. She had her hands around his neck and he was holding them very tightly.

Dill instinctively knew that these visions were something to do with sense and his parents had no idea that he was seeing them. He tried to alert them, but there was nothing he could do. When he went to call out to them, he realised that his words were frozen inside him.

He had a feeling of foreboding as he watched his mother get off her rock and slowly walk around the stones as if she was being pulled to the one on the other side of his father's stone. She was somehow connected to it. The boulder in her tummy had gone now, but although she wasn't speaking, he could hear her crying and calling out to God, telling him that she was so angry at him and that she wanted to have one more moment with her daughter. Her anger looked like a ball of fire raging in her chest.

Dill himself was now being drawn back towards his father, who had also moved and was now sitting on top of the stone his mother was holding on to. Legs crossed, he looked as if he was meditating, but Dill knew he wasn't at peace. He was angry too, but his anger was quiet and cold and deep, like a dark pool of water. Dill tried to look more deeply into the cold anger, but it ran into a dark watery ravine so deep that not even sense could tell where it ended.

Both his mother and father looked as though they'd been made to face something that was buried deep in their heart, and both were looking bewildered as his father slid off the stone and faced his mother without saying a word. They were now both standing by the same stone.

Dill knew that he couldn't leave them like this.

'Quickly, come and see this stone!'

The voice coming out of his mouth sounded like his own, but seemed to come from deep within him; it felt like Grandma's voice.

'How strange,' Dill thought, but he didn't have time to think about it further. He jumped from his stone, grabbed his parents' hands and pulled them towards the stone his grandma always sat on when she needed to think and feel better.

'Hurry,' he commanded.

Both of his parents put a foot on the large moss-covered boulder, and instantly a kind of electrical charge seemed to move through them and Dill could see their anger disappearing.

His mother began to babble. 'Oh, I got so dizzy there for a moment. You were right earlier calling me "old girl" – can't leap from stones any more without getting a head-rush, ha, ha, ha, ha!'

'I know what you mean,' his father replied. 'I was sitting there earlier, meditating like an old hippie, and I think I got that same buzz, ha, ha, ha!'

He was laughing really hard now and his mother was almost in hysterics, and Dill should have been the same, but he knew that something had happened that wasn't funny at all. Still, he didn't want to take away the sound of his parents laughing, even if it wasn't real laughter. He just had to get them back to Moon Cottage before anything else happened to them that he didn't have a clue about.

Luckily for him, Bramble saved the day with a great big mucky leap onto his father's commando trousers, which meant he would have to go home and change.

'Ha, ha, this crazy dog – I just love how unpredictable she is!'

His father was still laughing and his mother wasn't even upset about how dirty the dog was or the fact that she would have more washing to do. Dill just couldn't figure them out.

'OK, everybody home!' he called out as if he were the parent and they were the children and headed off in the direction of Moon Cottage.

He knew that he needed to talk to someone about his parents' moods and the only one he could share it all with was Jack Brabbit.

Chapter Eleven
The Mood Stones

Back at the cottage, Dill still felt a bit mixed up. What he had seen and felt had been strange enough, but even more perplexing was how calmly both his parents were behaving now, as if their minds had been wiped clean of everything that had happened. His father was talking about making one of his specials for supper, which meant that lots of food would get thrown into a pan and fried to death, leaving anyone who ate it with wind.

'Hey, Rosie, how about I *sauté* a few things in a kind of French fashion, pour in a little wine and we'll call it fun?'

'Yeah, well, as long as I can drink some of that wine, the food will be edible.'

She gave a kind of muffled snort into her sleeve.

'What, honey? Do you think that would be nice?'

'Nice? I think some wine would be fabulous, darling. Never mind the food, let's just start with a good glass to get us started, Tommy-boy.'

The world had turned upside down, Dill thought.

Even Bramble seemed to be caught up in the craziness; either that or she was just a great opportunist, as she was helping herself to her treats while his parents were laughing their heads off, applauding her efforts and calling out things like 'Nice one, Brams.'

It was definitely time to go and ask Jack if he could help him understand what was going on, Dill thought. Only first he'd better hide the treats from the dog before she burst.

Dill waited in his den with his torch in his hand. It was almost dusk, the time when the Brabbits would normally come out, but within seconds Jack and his two sisters had squeezed through the tunnel and were sitting by his side.

'Jack, you need to hear this,' Dill was saying in as clear a sense as he could produce when another rabbit head pushed into the den. It was Mrs Brabbit, and she seemed to be anxious to speak to him.

'Stop there, Dillan. I want you to start from the beginning and be as accurate and deliberate as possible when you bring this sense to us.'

There was something about Jack's mum at that moment that really reminded Dill of his grandma. He started to relate how his parents had been very happy and it had made him feel very happy and but then at the stones he had seen and heard things in sense and his parents had gone all funny.

'Dillan, stop!' Mrs Brabbit burst in. 'Slow down. Tell me more about the stones and anything that happened around that area.'

Dill could see what she wanted immediately. 'Mum was reluctant to go near the stones on our way out, but by the time we were on our way back she was quite happy to climb on them and play around on them like a child.'

He stopped for a moment and realised that the older rabbit was able to see and feel everything he wanted her to in a single moment.

'OK. Now, Dill, let me see what happened when you first walked past the stones, only slower please.'

He went back again to the moment and this time he could feel his mother's fear of being close to the standing stones. Mrs Brabbit was taking in every essence of the memory and, it would seem, understanding even more about it than he'd imagined he could reveal.

'OK,' she said, thoughtfully. 'Now slowly take me through the last part, where they both climbed onto the stones, only this time try not to remember it, just see it in your memory, please.'

She was doing something with her own mind that made it easy for Dill to produce sense and again he knew she was somehow able to completely understand what she was seeing, which was good because he still didn't have a clue what had happened.

The rest of the Brabbit family were huddled together and completely caught up in the sense memory too. The feeling in the den was intense, especially when Dill got to the part where he'd heard his grandma's voice and instinctively grabbed his parents' hands.

'You actions were correct, Dill,' Mrs Brabbit said. Her sense was gentler now. 'Your sense nature is what made you act the way you did; sense is a compassionate force and it works on our instinct, and when we don't get in the way of our instinct, we are working in harmony with Mother Nature. It was nature that made you take them to the healing stone.'

'What?'

'Dill, they got a blast of light from the healing stone and that's what has made them feel a little light in the head. It won't harm them – if anything, it will do them good to float for a while.'

She gave a cute little giggle that made her seem like her daughters for a moment.

'OK, I need to take this back to the burrow and go over it and then I'll come back and let you know what I think, Dill. Don't worry, everything will become clear. Oh, and girls, try to explain the stones to Dill. It will save me from doing it when I return.'

Droopsy wasted no time; she began to blab in her best sense. 'Sometimes the stones are called the feeling stones because if your feelings are all messed up you can go there and find the stone that will fix how you feel. It's amazing.'

Dill nodded at her and smiled. He loved watching her ears drooping down the sides of her face when she talked sense with him and her big dark eyes widening whenever she got excited.

Bunty took over from her sister. She was shorter and much rounder, and her nose twitched constantly when she was sensing.

'Some creatures call them the mood stones because they can reveal whatever mood a creature is in. And if your sense is very good or the air is thin, you can see into another creature's feelings and see what is causing their light body troubles.'

'Or hear them,' Jack cut in, which caused both of his sisters to drop their eyelids slowly at this untimely interruption.

Droopsy carried on, keen to show that she was in control. Fixing her big round eyes on Dill's, she told him, 'What the stones reveal to you is different in the time of each goddess, because each season affects our moods in different ways. So, what you see and what you feel in the time of one goddess can be entirely different from the next, which I think is sooo … amazing.'

'But,' her sister continued the moment Droopsy drew breath, 'no-sense creatures who sit or stand on the stones can become very confused, because they have things revealed to them that they didn't even know were inside them, and that is soo … what happened to your parents, I think.'

Droopsy's ears were now trailing on the ground as she explained, 'Every single stone will bring up different feelings, and beside each of the big stones there sits a small boulder. Once you've seen the feeling you wish to fix, or the mood you wish to change, that boulder has the power to make it better for you. And that's totally amazing too, isn't it?'

She looked around the den for agreement, but her sister ignored her attempts at getting attention and took over again. 'That is why the little ones are called the healing stones – because they fix things.'

'Or compassion stones, Mummy says,' Jack added, sticking his little tongue out at both his sisters. 'She says that the stones mean different things to different people and that's why there are so many names for them. They are magical and no one really knows what true power they have, so there.'

He sat up on his hind legs, looking proud of himself.

His mum was back in the den now and was tuning her sense to Dill's to see if he had understood. Using her very best sense abilities most deliberately, as she was aware that Dill was still very young and she knew that her words had to be appropriate, she explained, 'When my husband was taken from us I became confused, a bit uncertain about things, in much the same way that your parents have been since losing your sister. My light began to fade and nothing I did would bring it back. Dill, are you following me?'

He nodded.

She continued, 'I went to the stones to try to get answers about how I was feeling. Each stone has its own understanding of how to fix us, but we have to be truly ready to be fixed, Dill.'

Mrs Brabbit explained that all the creatures who were old enough to use the stones did so in times of need.

'Your grandma uses them. That is where we met and ... well, that's another story for another day. But the point is that your parents are lost in their feelings right now and they found themselves in a place that will be able to help them when the time is right, but it's not right at the moment, Dill, so all they got was a little lift. Now that doesn't mean that they won't get better in the future, but it does tell us that we must still be patient.'

She knew that Dill's next question would be about the power of the stones, so she let him know she would say more on it next. Dill listened patiently. He had stopped being amazed at the older sense creatures' ability to perceive the next moment.

'The first stone you stood on was the seeing stone, which reveals to anyone what they need to see at that particular time. In your case, Dill, when you saw the goddesses in the sky the first time you stood on it, it was because you were confused about sense and you wanted to understand what was happening to you. At that time you wouldn't have understood that, because you hadn't asked it in human words, but as you now know how to use sense, you will see that the stones respond to the inner language.'

She was right – it was beginning to make sense to Dill, especially as each sense explanation included pictures.

'When your mother was there that first time with you, she stood on the stone of change. The stone of change works best when we go to it asking how to change how we are at that time. When it reveals the answer, we can then spend time on its companion healing stone and begin to feel the direction of the change we have to make. It gives us courage to change.'

'But,' said Dill, 'when my mother stood on it, her feelings and thoughts were of the past. So, did she see something that she couldn't change? I thought she did, and that's why it hurt her and frightened her.'

'Exactly, Dill. If she'd known that a creature has to put their mind on what they want to change in the here and now when they stand on that stone, a very different picture might have come to her. But yes, sadly your mother saw something that she couldn't change.'

She dropped her head for a moment as if she was actually seeing what Dill's mother had seen and feeling what she'd felt. Dill was a little shaken by this. If he hadn't seen it or felt it that day, how could she feel it now?

Mrs Brabbit reassured him in a second. 'When you are able to know this, Dill, I promise you either your grandma or I will tell you in much more detail.'

She continued to give her findings, explaining that the stone that both his mother and father had climbed onto was the heart stone.

'Only one person can be on that stone for it to show their true heart, which is what it does, and by some instinct your mother left it and jumped onto the light stone. This reveals how much light is in your heart and what your light body looks like. That's why you saw for a moment what she was truly feeling inside.'

She shook her head and her long ears seemed to vibrate for a second or two after she had finished. Dill's head moved in the same way, as he reflected on what he'd seen.

Mrs Brabbit carried on, 'She feels as if she's carrying a great boulder that is both heavy and dark. Her light body is in that stone, and your father's heart is holding onto your sister, Dillan. When you saw him carrying her on his back, her hands may have been clasped around his neck, but his hands were unable to let go of her. He needs to feel the weight of her on his back to feel connected to her. His heart won't let go of her, that is what the heart stone revealed to you today, and if only he could have seen sense the way you do he would have understood that, but instead he did what he's been doing since she went to Light Land – he moved on but he didn't let go, he held the weight around his neck as a constant reminder of his pain.'

Dill felt for his father at that moment, and then for both his parents. As young as he was, he could see what they were suffering. He only wished that they saw it too.

His thoughts went to the next stone, the one his father had sat on and his mother had walked around, but Jack's mother was already telling him about it.

'Then they both connected with the truth stone, and this is the stone that shows us the truth of where we are when connect with it. Your poor father seems to be angry, but doesn't actually know whom to be angry with. He's put his anger so far inside himself that he's forgotten it exists. But sadly, it does.'

'But we can fix him, Mum, can't we?' Jack broke in. 'We can send more light and fix them both!'

'Yes!' the girls cried. 'We'll send all our light and do everything we can to lift them. Light always works. And...'

Their mother gave a sigh that said, 'Enough.' She looked around the group. 'We'll try everything we can, but let me continue now. Dill needs clarity in his thinking and I have to help him until Grandma Vi gets back, so just trust me, children, please.'

She gave a little wiggle of her nose and carried on.

'At least Dill's mother has a God to be angry with.'

A look of perplexity came from the Brabbit children at the word 'God' with no picture to accompany it, but a shrug from their mother told them to forget it and stay with her.

'The truth stone,' she continued, 'showed the anger of both your parents. One was hot and fiery, the other cold and deep. Anger is just anger, of course – it's what we do with it that makes it hot or cold – but we have more answers now, more idea of how to try to help them, Dill, and that is the most important thing just now. Thank the goddess that you put them on the healing boulder for the seeing stone – it was the effect of that stone that lifted their minds above the sad memories that they are carrying. Because there's no immediate solution to their problem, the best the stone could do was give them a boost to help them carry on until a solution appears.'

She told Dill that if he hadn't got them on the healing boulder they might have been left with all sorts of added confusions and problems, as they weren't ready to be healed or let go, and forcing the issue could have made the situation worse.

Dill got it, not in complete detail, but he understood without even knowing how he understood. Mrs Brabbit had made him feel better about the day. Even though he'd seen and felt much of his parents' pain and sorrow, at least he had a better understanding of it now.

Suddenly Jack spoke. 'Tell him about the sixth stone and the smaller one, the seventh small stone.'

His words reminded Dill that there were six big stones and seven little compassion boulders. He was very curious, but Mrs Brabbit said that she thought they'd talked enough sense for one night. She stopped sensing to them and sent out a shudder which seemed to go beyond the roof of the den, as if she was sensing someone else. Then she told the Brabbits it was time to go home.

As they went back down the tunnel, she stayed for a moment with Dill in the den and asked, 'How do you feel?'

There were no more pictures in her sense and he wasn't really sure what he had been asked.

'I'm – I'm OK, I think.'

'No, I want you to try to explain to me in sense what you're feeling, Dill. You were on those stones too and I sense that I need you to share what happened with me. If you can't right now, that's OK, but it might help things.'

They were alone in the den and Dill had no idea why, but he started slowly to explain his own feelings to the wonderful lady rabbit who was sitting on the ground opposite him.

'I did feel heavy today before we went out – as if I didn't have much light, I think.'

Mrs Brabbit stayed silent. Her eyes were actually closed, as she could see sense without looking.

'Then,' Dill continued, 'I was angry. I was angry at my parents for not trying to get better and for always blaming each other when neither of them wants to talk about the right things, they just keep fighting about the wrong things – anything, I don't know.'

Words were flowing from him and he wasn't sure if he was speaking, thinking or sensing, but he couldn't stop now.

'I know that they're sad, but *I'm* sad too, I lost my sister who used to play with me at video games and who was with me on holidays and who stole things from me and always wanted more attention from my parents than me, but nobody ever asks me if I'm sad, so I just talk to myself or Bramble, and I don't want to be sad, but I don't want not to be, because I don't want to forget Amber. But I don't want them to forget *me* – I didn't die, I'm still here, I'm not in heaven, I'm right here in front of them and they just don't see me.'

There was a tension, an energy, in the little den. The rabbit knew that it had to be released from the boy. She saw his own burden, which was like thunder and lightning about to burst. This was what he was doing now: letting it rain out of him. Her knowledge of nature told her that when the atmosphere got like this, it had to rain to clear the air.

Dill was crying quietly, wiping the tears from his face with the backs of his hands. He looked directly at Mrs Brabbit.

Sitting up as tall as she could, she looked straight back at him.

'How do you feel now, Dill?'

Her sense was soothing and comforting and there was healing in her very tone.

He took a deep breath and said, 'I do feel better, but I'm sorry...'

She shushed him and gave the biggest genuine sense smile she could muster.

'Son, there are things being done that I can't share with you yet, but I promise you that things are being done. Now go and rest. Oh, and keep your parents away from the stones until your grandma gets back. You've done well today, Dill, but now it's time for bed, and remember, the new day will bring new solutions.'

With those words, she spun round and dashed back through the little hole in the wall.

Dill headed back across the twilight garden. His head was clearer now and he felt as though something had been released from him. But what had she meant by 'things are being done'?

His didn't notice the shadowy figure who had been sitting on the wall just beside the roof of his den. Alice Otus lifted her wings silently and, with no effort at all, glided in the direction of the moonlit wish tree.

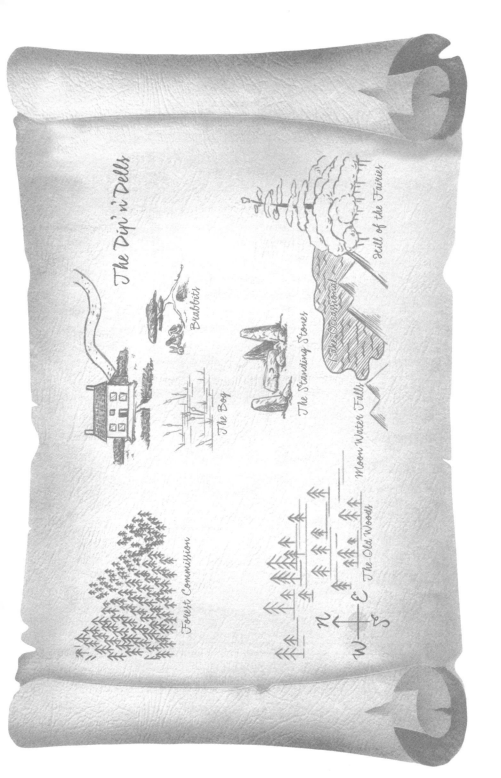

Chapter Twelve
The Meeting of Old and New

Springtime was now in full show over the dells and there was a high energy and sense of activity that filled the air with a living motion. All of the creatures were enjoying the new arrivals born in the time of the young goddess.

Dill was studying for the postal exams that his mother had gained permission from the education department for him to sit, as she didn't want him to miss out on the normal curriculum for his age group, even though she still wanted to stay out of town and away from other parents just now. Dill was very bright, and his understanding of sense was helping him to see things plainly and clearly in his everyday life. Really, the stuff he had to study was quite easy for him.

His grandma had been back with them for over three weeks now, but had been out of the house so much on her own that Dill was feeling a bit cut off from her. She would be out early in the morning before anyone got up and some nights didn't arrive home before he went to sleep. He knew that something was going on and wanted her to let him in on it, but the old lady was having none of it. All she would say was, 'All in good time, Dill, all in good time.'

Despite Grandma being absent so much, the days and nights passed very quickly for Dill and Jack. They often spent time outdoors now, as the weather was much better and the days stayed light for much longer. They only really used the den when it was raining, which it had been for the first week of April. But now the sun was a bit more permanent in the sky and playtimes seemed much longer, which somehow made time redundant.

Jack was now very fond of Bramble too and she spent much of her time making all the Brabbits laugh by playing chasing games with them around the bog at the back of Moon Cottage.

Dill could hear the sense laughter in the garden now. Bramble was chasing Jack, and Bunty and Droopsy were in hysterics.

'I always thought Bramble was a hunting dog – aren't spaniels used for flushing out game?'

His father was rubbing his head in disbelief as he watched from the kitchen window. The big spaniel was bouncing round after a tiny rabbit who was literally running rings around her.

'Rose, come and see this. Honestly, our dog's rubbish at catching things.'

His wife was ironing clothes from a big pile on the chair beside her.

'Busy. Can't you see I've got lots to do? Can't just stand around and watch a dog chase a rabbit.'

'I know, but this is silly. It's actually quite funny. Look, stop that and come and watch this.'

'I said I was busy, now just leave it, would you, unless you want to do the ironing.'

There was a hush and even the animals outside seemed to catch the mood and stopped their game.

Without a word, Dill's father went out.

Dill was still concerned about his parents, and not just because they were having a little tiff. When he'd tried to tell his grandma the things he'd witnessed at the stones, she'd just told him that she understood and that all would be well in time. It wasn't like her to shut him out, he thought, and he wondered what she'd been doing at her old place, because she'd brought back loads of stuff in big cases, but every time he asked her about it, she just became more secretive.

Once he'd known that she was sensing with Alice by the shed, but she'd dismissed it, saying that she was just saying hello as she passed by. But he knew those two old birds were hiding something, and he wanted to know what it was. It troubled him that there was something so private that he couldn't know about it. Maybe it was something really bad.

He'd been almost certain that they were doing something for his parents, but if that was the case it should be a good thing. Why couldn't he help with it? Why did the older ones assume he wouldn't be able to handle things the way they did?

'Stop thinking and carry on studying, Dill,' his grandma called out to him.

His mother looked up from the ironing board with a quizzical expression on her face. How could she know he wasn't studying?

Grandma had just plonked herself in the new rocking chair she'd brought back with her, looking quite pleased with herself after her early morning excursion.

'If you're wondering where Bramble is, she's with your father down by the standing stones.'

Dill couldn't help but worry when he heard that, but Grandma winked at him.

'It's alright. I suggested it to him earlier. Why don't we go down as well, Rose?'

Dill's mother looked up.

'Maybe later, Mother. You can see that I'm up to here with things and I really should carry on, but you go out and enjoy the walk with Tom, he seems a bit edgy this morning.'

Dill looked up in total disbelief – *she* had been the edgy one!

'No, dear,' his grandma said firmly. 'I insist that you come. It's because you've been so busy that I want to take you for a walk. You deserve a break, Rose.'

This was too strange, Dill thought. He was going to have to enlist the help of his friend and his two sisters to try to find out what the oldies were planning.

Out in the garden Dill could feel Jack's presence and knew he was waiting for him in the den. Before he could ask him if he had any info on what was going on, though, Jack said, 'OK, you were right, Dill, something's going down tonight over by the mood stones.'

Excitement ran through Dill's entire body. 'How d'you know?'

Jack hurriedly continued, 'One of the badger cubs I know, called Baggy, was out foraging by the stones last night and he picked up the sense conversation between my mother, your grandma and Alice the long-eared owl.'

Dill's blue eyes were widening with anticipation. 'Go on, go on. And...?'

'And he said they were talking about a special event in the time of Lassaisha – you know, the summer goddess – and Alice Otus mentioned an offering of some kind that would be very risky and Baggy knew this to be true because he could feel a sense of danger in what they were saying.'

Jack's long ears were now pointing straight above his little head, his two front teeth were hanging over his lower lip and his eyes were bulging.

Dill's eyes were also popping out. 'So when is the special event? What are they going to do?'

'I don't know, but they're going to have a meeting tonight and they'll discuss their plans then, don't you see? The standing stones are probably their headquarters. And we can have Baggy-boy down there spying for us.'

There was something about those stones, Dill thought. 'What do you know about the sixth one?' he asked.

Jack told him that when it came to life, it was said to have more power than the wish tree.

'Power to do what?' asked Dill. 'And when does it come to life?'

He was sure that what the older women were planning had something to do with that, and Jack could feel it too.

But Dill also knew that his grandma wouldn't tell them anything, and Jack had already tried to quiz his mum and she'd clammed up completely.

The youngsters decided to enrol Jack's sisters into their group, as they felt that they might get more out of their mum than he could.

It was pointless trying to sneak out anywhere near the stones during the meeting – the old ladies had too much sense for that – so Jack would also ask Baggy to find out what he could and fill them in the following morning.

'The girls should come to the meeting too and see if they can help fill in any of the missing gaps,' Dill suggested.

'Great – we're both thinking the same thing at the same time. This means that our sense is connected and really boosted, Dill.'

'Yeah, I feel it too,' Dill agreed. 'Between all of us, we'll get to the bottom of this.'

He told Jack that his grandma had sent his father to the stones with the dog and was planning on taking his mother there also.

'Could we use Bramble to spy?' Jack wondered.

'No, not a good idea, Jack, because she is far too easy to get things out of. But let's see what Baggy can tell us tomorrow!'

Dill had spent so long in the den that when he went back into the house there was no one there. He decided that this was a good time to look for clues in his grandma's room.

A quick glance around it told him that there was nothing to be learned there, though. All the large cases were locked and all that was on view was a big book with the words *This Year's Astronomy* written on the front of it. Smiling at how cunning his old grandma was, he went into the kitchen for a snack.

Halfway through munching a thick cheese sandwich he'd made for himself, he noticed that Bramble was standing on the wall of the garden, her long tongue hanging out, looking back over the dells. That meant his parents were coming back, but his sense told him that something wasn't right.

His father was first to come through the break in the wall, but he was holding his mother with one arm.

'Hey, come on. It's OK, love,' he was saying.

Instinctively Dill ran to the back door.

Grandma was right behind them and rubbing his mother's back.

'Come now, Rose, let's get a nice cup of tea inside you.'

Dill could see that his mother was sobbing; even his father looked as though he was crying. He stood and watched as the three adults hugged in the middle of the garden. There were flowers from the dells in his mother's hand. What was going on?

It was only when he heard his grandma's voice saying, 'It's only natural, it's her birthday, darling,' that he realised that today was 12th April, his sister's birthday, and it was the first birthday without her.

He was rooted to the ground, frozen like a statue for a moment. Then he ran to his mother. Forcing his way into the hug, he tried to give all his light to her through his body.

Then he remembered his father's sadness, and pulled tightly on his waist so that they were all connected. He thought that between him and his grandmother there would be enough light to fix both parents.

For a moment it seemed to be so, but then his father pulled away and said, 'I'd better go in and feed the dog. She must be starving.'

As he spoke, Dill could feel his deep ravine of anger.

His mother, though, was softening. 'Sorry, Dill, Mum,' she whispered. 'I honestly never expected it. But I do feel good about picking flowers for Amber. She would have loved it here.'

She let out another sob.

'Darling,' his grandmother said to her, 'you have to let it out or it will hurt more in the long run. Well done.'

She hugged her daughter tightly, breaking more of the stiffness that was holding her rigid.

She was releasing something in his mother, Dill realised. It reminded him of the night when Mrs Brabbit had allowed him to release something in himself.

It was passing now, but he knew that this was probably one of the most difficult moments of spring for him and his family.

It took a couple of days for Dill's parents to get back to some kind of normality, and that was mostly down to being in the garden more now than in the house. The weather was improving all the time.

'Yes, winter can be tough in the dip 'n' dells. Many things are covered up in winter and spring really does allow us all to see the truth, as everything is released and is allowed to break through. It's the things that break through that have a chance to continue. But then you know that.'

Grandma was talking to her roses as she watered them. She had pruned them back a few weeks ago and now new shoots were beginning to form.

His father raised his eyes from his newspaper, looked at his mother-in-law and slowly shook his head.

Dill smiled.

'Anyone fancy some ice cream?' his mother asked. 'I think it's just hot enough for it today.'

Everyone said yes at the same time and she headed for the kitchen.

There hadn't been many, but this was a day of peace and relaxation in the house, or rather outside the house. Brigisha was at her height and it was difficult not to be affected by the giddy sense of springtime on a day like this.

Bramble was lying in the shade of the den with her big tongue hanging out. She lifted one ear and tilted her head to one side to listen to something within the den, then relaxed, as she knew that who she was sensing was a friend.

The youngsters had met several times in the den over springtime, but nothing much had come of it. Grandma had postponed her meeting at the stones on the night of Amber's birthday and as yet nothing had come back from Baggy about a new meeting. The girls were doing well at playing dumb around their mother, but were still none the wiser. Dill and Jack had put together a theory of what was being planned, but it was based only on the fact that when one had a good idea the other would immediately sense the same thing.

'OK, Jack, Grandma has brought lots of things back with her that she is keeping locked away and they could be things the stag would like.'

'Right, so maybe she's going to bribe the stag to allow your parents to attend the next gathering. And that will help them get their light back. It's so clear, I'm telling you!'

Jack was quite sure of himself and it was obvious to Dill that he was right.

'Yes,' he said, 'and the reason it's risky is that if the other elders, like the eagle or the old hare, get wind of it, they'll all be had up on a charge of corruption. Maybe that's why Alice Otus is involved.'

'Of course it is! She's the best legal mind in the dells. She's probably behind everything. It was her, I bet, who made contact with the Lord of the Dells. She could get to him. Yeah, that's it. She could also defend Grandma Vi if it all goes bad.'

It all made sense, but the thing was, it had all gone so quiet now that there was nothing to sense.

And yet the atmosphere in the dells was getting thinner; it was only a few days before the arrival of the summer goddess and the next gathering, which was to be on the banks of Lake Occasional.

Early one evening Bramble was in the garden playing with a battered old stick while Dill watched her through the window. Suddenly, she looked over at the den and Dill knew that Jack needed him to come. Even before the dog could turn towards him, he was out of the door.

Pulling back the tarpaulin, he found Jack, his two sisters and a small badger he assumed was Baggy. He now knew why they called the poor animal this: it was because his furry coat looked four sizes too big for him and hung in a way that made it seem that he was carrying lead weights in side pockets.

'Has something happened?'

By the look of excitement on Jack's face he knew it had.

'It's tonight!' Jack beamed. 'They're all gonna be there – Grandma Vi, Mum and Alice have all agreed to meet by the stones to discuss their plan.'

He looked so pleased with himself, but poor Baggy wanted to talk. After all, he was the one who had got the info.

'Em, *sniff*, I, eh, *sniff*…'

Baggy always seemed to have a runny nose; even in sense it still came out like that.

'Yeah, we know, Baggy,' Jack said quickly.

Then even louder sniffing sounds were heard from the other side of the tarpaulin. It was Bramble.

'Quick, Grandma Vi is coming!'

Dill shot out of the den to give the others time to disappear before his grandma got a sense of them. He especially wanted the badger gone, or she might put two and two together.

'Hi, Grandma, where've you been today?' he asked, trying to put his thoughts and feelings as far away from his mind as possible.

She smiled at him and said nonchalantly, 'Oh, just in my room, Dill, catching up on some reading. What have you been up to?'

'Oh, nothing much. I was just talking to Jack, but he had to go home. His mother wanted him or something.'

'Did she?'

Dill knew that he had to get away because he was so full of questions that he could feel them rising inside him and his grandmother was bound to catch on.

'Need the loo, Grandma Vi – I mean Grandma!' he shouted in a desperate sort of voice as he dashed for the house.

She watched him leave and smiled over at the corner of the garden where Mrs Brabbit was sitting. The little rabbit scrunched up her nose in an attempt to smile back.

Alice looked down from the roof of Moon Cottage. 'They know nothing, Vi.'

She gave a shrill kind of laugh, then rolled her wings back over her shoulders and winked before launching herself into the still evening air.

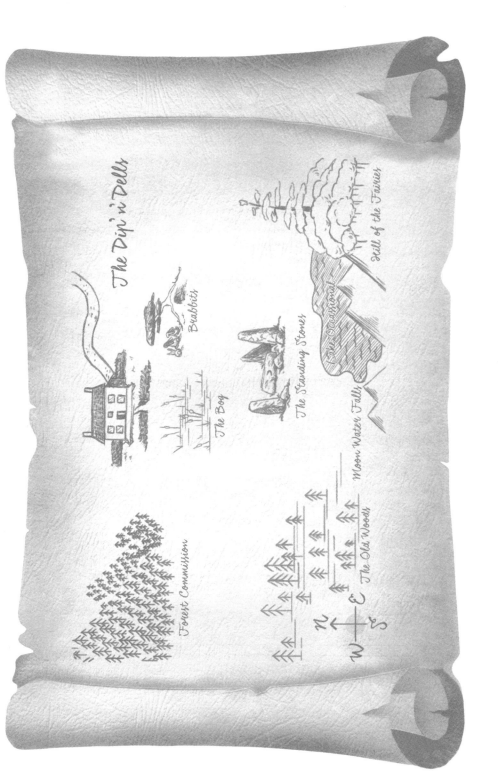

The Dip' n' Dells

Forest Commission

Brabbits

The Bog

The Standing Stones

Four Deathmist

Moon Water Falls

Hill of the Fairies

The Old Woods

N E S W

Chapter Thirteen
Summertime Settles

Lassaisha is the epitome of summer: she is warm, like the sun, and very giving, like the Earth in her season. Her stay is a relaxing one after the turbulence of Brigisha's ups and downs; Lassaisha is slower, mellower, and brings elegance to the air she occupies. She is there to help and heal; it is in her time that much of the natural world finds balance and tranquillity. If the young spring goddess brings things to the surface, then her more mature counterpart makes sense of them and gives reasons for all of the difficulties that have gone before. She rewards all those who have struggled to get to her season by providing them with peace. It's hard not to recognise the wonders of the world on a warm summer's day with all of nature's gifts on full display. Many things are settled in the summertime, because the goddess of summer is at peace with all of life and even the natural elements respect her grace and lessen their force when she is present.

She also reminds us that just as the warmth of the summer sun can burn away the clouds in the sky, so the bright mind can disperse the doubts and fears that try to form around it. Her nature is to shine light into all the darkest corners. She achieves this by keeping the world lighter for longer each day of her stay. Her energy is strong and she is always relaxed, but doesn't need much sleep.

On the night before her arrival, Dill's father couldn't sleep. He was sitting in his little office next to his son's bedroom not knowing what to do with himself. He had been having so many sleepless nights lately and so many crazy dreams that were bitty and abstract and left him feeling that there were messages there that he couldn't grasp.

He shook his head and then leaned back on the padded leather seat and pushed both his hands through his thick brown hair. Resting his hands on the back of his head, he began to take deep breaths to try and relax. His body *was* relaxed, but his head was a mishmash of disjointed thinking.

One thought took him back to his job, to the noisy open-plan accounts office he'd shared with more than 50 people. He remembered the babble of dozens of phone conversations and the humming and buzzing of the machines and the effort it took not to get washed away in the wave of unimportant noise. Here there was no background noise at all – well, not much. He stopped his train of thought to listen for a moment. Somewhere in the distance he could hear birds calling out to one another. He didn't know what they were, but he was sure his son did. He smiled at the memory of Dill identifying the birds by Lake Occasional.

But that memory seemed to disturb something in him; it touched a part of him that he wasn't ready to look at. The memory of his son's voice had found a memory of his daughter's voice and released it from deep inside him.

'Daddy, I love you so, so much. You are my big daddy and I'll never let you go.'

Sitting there in the stillness of the little room, he clasped his hands in front of his chest as if he was holding something tight – and he was. It was the memory of when he'd last played with his daughter before the cancer had made her too weak. It was his most precious memory and he'd locked it away inside himself so that no one could take it from him.

He wasn't ready to deal with this. Wiping his eyes, he stood up. He couldn't sit here any longer in the wee small hours when his mind was vulnerable.

'You will do what all accountants do when they can't sleep,' he told himself. 'You will go to bed and count someone else's money till you drop off.'

Dill was up early the next morning. He couldn't wait to go out to his den to hear the news of the meeting between his grandmother and her cronies. The feeling of anticipation building in him matched perfectly with the thick, electrically charged air around the dip 'n' dells. It would soon be time for the goddesses to change over.

There was a definite feeling of unease in the kitchen. His mother was sitting on his grandmother's rocking chair, rocking back and forwards and gnawing her nails. She looked exhausted.

'Dill, you can play in the garden if you've finished with your food. I'll come out later when I've showered.'

'Is Dad awake, Mum?'

Dill wanted to know if his parents were likely to disturb his meeting with his friends.

'No, he couldn't sleep again, so he's, well, he's still asleep. Don't disturb him. Grandma and the dog are out somewhere. Go and join them if you want.'

Dill stood for a second looking at his mother's tired expression and wished that he could give her some of his energy, but instinct pulled him towards the back door.

In the den, Dill, Jack and the girls were listening to the little badger.

'I was there, *sniff*, around midnight, *sniff*. There wasn't much moon, so I know it was late. *Snirrff.*'

'Yeah, Baggy, we get the picture,' Jack broke in. 'Guess what, Dill? The stag was standing there with them.'

'No! You saw him, Baggy?' Dill was stunned. The bribe!

Then Dropsy Brabbit burst in, her ears moving up and dropping down. 'I saw with my own eyes our mother sneak through the tunnel leading into the den, where she was picked up by Grandma Vi and they headed towards the stones, so that is like confirmation of what Baggy says. It's amazing.'

Not to be outdone, Bunty squealed, 'That's so true, because I waited up but pretended to be asleep when I sensed my mummy's presence and I could sense the last conversation between her and Grandma Vi, which ended with Mummy telling Grandma Vi that she would be right behind her when the time came.'

Dill's thoughts were racing so much that he couldn't think in any one straight line.

Then Baggy added, 'Alice told your grandmother at the end of the meeting that when she made the offer it was binding and it could not be called off and then your grandmother accepted that it was a deal. Snirrrff.'

Then even louder sniffing sounds were heard from the other side of the tarpaulin once more. Bramble!

But this time she was followed by Grandma.

'Off you go,' she said quickly to the dog. 'Run around to keep all sense creatures away from this meeting.'

Bramble disappeared.

'Right, all of you,' Grandma said, 'I'm here to tell you that, as you have guessed, or should I say sensed, there is a plan to help Dill's parents.'

'I told you, Dill!' Jack was up on his hind legs, bursting with excitement.

'Hush, Jack,' his mother said, and just in time. Bunty and Droopsy, who had also risen up on their hind legs, subsided without a word.

The children were sure that they were about to hear the bribe story now, but they didn't.

'I want you all to listen very carefully,' Grandma continued. 'Dill and I will be making a trip to the wish tree today. As you know, the goddess Lassaisha will take over tomorrow and this is the last day we have to leave our wish before her thin place happens and our wish can be considered. I think you all know what the wish will be and who it is for.'

Everyone nodded.

'Making this wish come true depends on everyone's full cooperation and trust.'

She stopped, expecting questions, but none came. Excitement was waning. Was that all it was? What about all the bribery and corruption?

'When we know more or feel that we can share more details with you, we will,' Grandma concluded, 'but in the meantime we don't want you going round putting out sense messages about conspiracies, as you never know who can tune into your sense out here. This is a delicate matter and could upset some of the creatures of the dells, so you must always trust us. Is that clear?'

'Yes, Grandma Vi,' the young Brabbits chorused, and Dill gave a good sense nod of the head.

With that, Grandma left the den and Mrs Brabbit and the girls disappeared down the tunnel.

Jack and Dill looked at each other.

'OK, Dill, so there wasn't any bribery and our theory wasn't close, but we weren't wrong about the old ladies planning something.'

'No, we weren't, were we?'

Jack got a little bit puffed up again and his cheeks began to swell.

'Think it was Baggy who knocked us off course, Jack.'

His friend nodded so fast that his teeth rattled. 'That's it, Dill. I was feeling the same thing.'

There was a kind of buzz beginning to build in the boys. Dill felt a warm glow at the thought of going to the wish tree later that day.

'It's the kind of excitement you get before the school holidays,' he thought.

'I have no idea what that was I just saw in your mind, Dill!'

The little rabbit looked bewildered at Dill's memory of his school, but rather than explain it today, Dill just laughed.

And Jack laughed too.

Dill and his grandma walked in the midday sun towards the hill of the fairies. It was warm, but the air was heavy and sticky and smelled of sweet perfume. Grandma was carrying a piece of white ribbon with 'Amber' written on it.

'The gathering is by the far end of the lake tomorrow and begins just when the sun comes up,' Grandma was saying as they approached the standing stones. Instinct made her stop and sit on her usual boulder.

'Will we see the last of the struggle between the goddesses grandma?'

'Well, there's not so much of a struggle at this one. Poor Brigisha is so exhausted at the end of her time that she simply collapses back into the Earth and Lassaisha graciously walks in. It's all very beautiful and exciting, though, the way they all are.'

Grandma thought back to her last thin place by the lake. She had been just three years older than Dill was now. Rowena had been with her; they had snuggled together on the bank of the lake and marvelled at the beauty of the summer goddess. They knew the season was all about settling things and bringing balance back to the dells and all who lived there. It was a happy time.

'What happened to Rowena, Grandma?'

She suddenly remembered that her grandson could share her memories and snapped out of her reverie.

'Oh, yes, well, she was of the age to start her young adult life and so was I, Dill. We knew that our lives would take us in different directions. We accepted that and even though we knew it would hurt to leave each other, it was the right thing.'

This was hard for Dill to understand. The old lady could feel it and tried to clarify things for the boy.

'You see, Dill, if this place teaches us anything, it is that life isn't easy. Nature is in charge here. Actually, nature is in charge everywhere – people just don't always understand that. They assume that they are in charge of their destiny and make plans to do one thing or another. And when their plans don't come off, more often than not, they fall apart. The human spirit gets broken when it doesn't get what it wants, and also when it has to yield to nature, but it has to do that eventually. We all have to surrender our hard body to nature at some point.'

Dill nodded as he digested all the sense she was sharing. He knew there was more to come too.

'You see, Dill, the goddesses represent change, as you have learned. They each remind us that nothing is permanent and that life has many different facets. This helps us to move on and not get stuck on one thing. It helps us to grow and expand when we open our awareness to the many things that are in our world other than ourselves.'

Grandma paused and checked to see if he was following her, and he was.

'In the place where we used to live, so many dreams get forgotten. So many people live without hope or belief and never for a minute think about the magic that is in the world here.'

She looked around her at the wonderful scenery and took in as much as her mind would allow.

'Here, even the air is filled with magic. And if there's even a chance that that magic can help your parents, then I'm going to try and make it happen with every ounce of power in my bodies, light and hard.'

Dill could really feel the power of his grandma at that moment; she was swelling with light. Her force moved through him and his eyes widened.

'Come, let's walk on. We'll share more at the tree.' She stood up nimbly and began to walk at a good old pace towards the lake. 'Bramble, come on, girl, we're off.'

Bramble leapt out of the long grass. She was crinkling and laughing hysterically as she shot out in front of them, and they could hear her talking sense to herself.

'Oh, that ruddy hedgehog cracks me up. Ha, ha, ha!'

As they walked, Dill wanted to know more about the sixth stone. He had forgotten to ask about it when they were sitting at the stones.

Grandma was on it at once. 'Ah, the moon stone. Everything I know about that stone is legend, but who knows, it may be true. It is said to lie dormant until something strange or rare happens to the moon.'

'What, like an eclipse?'

The old lady stopped in her tracks.

'Yes, like an eclipse.'

For a moment Dill thought he felt something strange in her energy, but she was already getting back into her stride. He must have been mistaken.

As they approached the lake, though, he had to ask, 'What happens then, when an eclipse comes? What happens to the stone?'

Still trotting forward, she replied, 'Remember, I don't know this for certain, but it is said that when there's a solar eclipse, that is, when the moon completely covers the sun, and day becomes night for a time, the moon stone becomes active. And when the moon stone becomes active, it creates a very special thin place where magical things beyond our wildest dreams can happen.'

Dill wondered what kind of magic could be more spectacular than the thin place he'd witnessed in the old wood and what he'd seen when Jack had shared his memories of the hill of the fairies gathering.

'But remember, Dill,' his grandmother cautioned, 'this is only a legend. No one has experienced these magical things, as a solar eclipse hasn't happened here for many, many years. Look, see those geese on Lake Occasional? They have come here to feed on their way north.'

'Yes, I see them.'

Lake Occasional was now much reduced, but Dill could see fluffy white clouds reflected in the water. He realised that they had come out of nowhere.

'Everything does change here, doesn't it, Grandma? But that's OK, I like it that way.'

She smiled. She was pleased that his mind, too, was agile enough to keep moving and not get stuck on any one thing, especially, at the moment, on the stones.

'Grandma, why are there 13 stones? Is there a reason?'

She laughed to herself. So much for diverting his mind!

'There are 13 moons in a dells year,' she said.

'Maybe they are all called the moon stones then. Everybody seems to have different names for them, like mood stones and feelings stones – maybe they're really called moon stones?'

Dell waited for a response to come back. His grandma seemed to be panting a bit.

'Yes, Dill, I think you have a point there, dear.'

'And why has the moon stone got two boulders at its foot while all the others only have one?'

'Oh, no one really knows and I suppose we will never find out unless the moon stone gets activated. Now do let me concentrate on where I'm walking, Dill, there's a good boy.'

Dill had been so involved in questioning his grandma that he hadn't realised that they were already walking up the hill of the fairies. He had never come this far from home. He stopped for a moment to take in his surroundings.

Tight beds of nettles acted as protectors at the foot of the hill, giving the area an almost eerie feel, but then, as the land rose and the trees became taller and more spaced out, it felt more peaceful. Like the rest of the dells, the hill was full of ditches and mounds, and some of the ground was wet and had little streams flowing down it, while other parts were dry and arid.

It must have taken 15 minutes to get to the circle of Scots pine trees that surrounded the magnificent wish tree at the top of the hill. Gazing up at it, Dill felt tiny in comparison.

'Wow, Grandma, this is amazing.'

'Yes, I know.'

She was laughing under her breath, and the sound was so infectious that Dill laughed too.

'Now will you tie this white ribbon to that big branch dropping down from the wish tree?'

Dill wondered why, but she ignored his sense for now. Instead she made a wish in sense, wishing that his parents might be free of their darkness.

Then she asked, 'Please may I be allowed to leave this wish with you so that the summer goddess may grant it?'

Dill felt her wish and it made him feel strong inside. He wished the same.

Then Grandma tied another piece of ribbon with writing on it to another branch and bowed her head slightly to the tree.

Finally, she took something that looked like birdseed out of her pocket and scattered it around the roots of the tree.

'Dill, take a walk around here and just feel the essence of the place. It is very special, you know.'

Dill started walking, but he noticed that his grandma didn't walk around herself. Instead, she knelt before the great tree as if in prayer to it. She might really have been praying to it, he thought, because he could no longer link to her sense.

He stood for a moment and watched her as she got up, took another piece of ribbon from her pocket and tied it to a higher branch. Then she touched the trunk of the tree with deep affection and stood there in silence.

Dill found a flat stone to sit on and allowed his mind to find Jack's memories of the hill when it had been made thin by Cailasha. He could see in his mind what it had looked like then: covered with creatures of every description. 'Out of this world,' he thought.

He'd seen the sparkling lights from a distance that night, but now he could actually feel the spectacle. It seemed to be lifting him until he thought he was floating.

'Wow!'

He rose so high that suddenly he thought he might fall. His eyes shot open and he pushed his hands forcefully down on the rock beneath him just to be sure it was there.

His grandma laughed and said, 'You must learn never to limit your sense feelings, Dill. One limited thought will bring you back to Earth with a bang.'

Dill laughed too. He hadn't really understood her words, but her mood was light.

They remained silent for a time just taking in the atmosphere of the magical place. When the sun broke through the trees, it lit up the ground with a strange glow. The little plants and shrubs burst into colour and the air was filled with tiny flying things that moved like clouds though the dense air. The tree trunks shone bright orange and their huge roots looked like long tendrils snaking across the ground. It was almost sinister in a way, and Dill wondered if it had to be like that to keep people away; only sense creatures would feel beyond what was scary and see the real beauty of the place.

'Grandma, why did you throw birdseed at the tree after you made your wish?'

'Well, I learned from my own grandmother that if you ask for something to be granted by Mother Nature then you must make an offering of some kind.'

She went to continue, but the boy carried on instead: 'So the seed would feed some of her creatures and a kind of balance would be made?'

The old lady was impressed. 'Yes, Dill, there always needs to be a balance in nature. Nothing is for nothing. Giving and receiving are from the same scale; they just lie at different ends.'

Dill was silent, but he totally understood what his grandma had told him. He was looking out over the dells and thinking how beautiful they were. He could see Bramble running around the lake at the bottom of the hill. She hadn't joined them, she was too busy off on her own pursuits. He smiled as he watched her playing so happily and realised how much he cared for her. He could see the stones too. How small they were from up here. In the distance he could see Moon Cottage and that was smaller still.

A group of crows was cawing above his head and he sensed that they were talking about him; Jack said no one in the dells had been able to stop talking about him and Grandma since the spring gathering.

'If they're talking about us, Dill, they're leaving someone else alone.'

Grandma gave a little laugh of reassurance, which pleased him. He felt able to ask what he really wanted to know.

'If our wish is accepted, will it mean that Mum and Dad will be able to come to the hill at the autumn gathering? Only it seems a long way off – I wish they could get help sooner. Can't they?'

His grandmother looked at him and tried to be as honest as she could.

'Dill, I am trying something which I can't talk to you about, but please trust me. When I can say more I will, but for now just let it be.'

As they approached the stones again on the way back to Moon Cottage, Dill wondered why his grandma had taken his parents there on Amber's birthday.

She felt his confusion and explained that she had needed to clear certain emotions from both of them before she made the wish.

As Dill's mind quizzed this, she explained, 'You know how it was when Mrs Brabbit shared your memories in the den? She felt something that she couldn't explain. It is difficult for a rabbit to totally understand human emotions, so I had to try to see it for myself. I had to know exactly how they were feeling.'

Dill understood. He was beginning to learn that when his grandma kept him in the dark, it was because she didn't have the whole picture yet.

'Dill, the first time you went to the stones with your mother, she reacted badly. She stood on the stone of change that day. Now, Jack's mother explained that to you, didn't she?'

Dill nodded, remembering.

'Sadly for your mother, she saw something that she wasn't able to change. On Amber's birthday I got her to place some flowers on the stone for her and she touched it with her hand. At that moment, I saw that she wished that she'd brought Amber to the dells for her last days.

She'd wanted to do it, but a part of her kept hoping that if she stayed in hospital a new cure would come or a treatment would be developed, and to take her so far away was like saying she had no chance.'

There was a pain in the boy's chest as he felt his mother's pain and the weight of her decisions.

'That's awfully sad, Grandma. I didn't know that Amber might have come here. It could have been…'

He stopped.

Grandma stood beside him and took his hand. She could see in his eyes that he understood.

'When someone we love dies, there are always too many "should haves" and "could haves". Your mother loved her daughter and would have offered her own life for hers if she could have, and therefore she has no need to feel guilty on top of all the other confusing emotions she has to deal with.'

Grandma spoke with real force and Dill realised why – she was standing by the heart stone and he could feel the fight in her heart when she spoke about her daughter.

She shook her head, aware that he knew what she was feeling, and laughed her knowing laugh once more. She placed her arm around Dill's shoulder and they slowly continued their walk back towards Moon Cottage.

'I always thought Amber would be the one who came here and learned sense,' she said. 'I was taught it by my grandmother, as you know, and I just assumed it would be the same.'

Her mind was showing Dill pictures of Amber and herself walking in the dells as she was doing with him right now. He knew she was thinking that she should be there with them.

'She is, Grandma,' he said. 'Her light body is with us all the time.'

The old lady smiled. She was happy he thought this way, the dells way.

'Grandma, we have to help Dad too. He's really suffering.'

'I know, son, I know.'

The sound of silence in their heads drowned out the calls of the animals and birds as dusk began to settle beneath the fiery sky. Nothing, it seemed, could disturb their walking contemplation. Nothing, that is, except a great big dirty, wet out-of-breath, springer spaniel leaping out of the thick heather.

'Your mother will go mad,' Grandma said as she looked at the black and muddy dog.

'I'm so sorry. I couldn't help myself, I just forgot.' Bramble's tongue was practically on the ground. Thankfully she was talking sense.

'Well,' Grandma said firmly, 'I think it's a bucket of water for you, lady!'

Bramble's head sank so low that it was almost trailing along the ground. She didn't need sense to see what was coming her way.

Bramble did get the bucket of water and she was confined to the back porch until dry, but Dill had a treat waiting for him that night: he was being taken to town by his parents to have pizza. He thought a lot about what his parents were going through on the drive home, and even though they were telling him they would do more with him in their happiest voices, he knew that in their hearts they were still battling with regrets over his sister's illness. They had no idea, but their young son really did understand where they were.

It was a strange thing for Dill, but he knew he could have helped them if only they'd spoken to him about what they were going through. After all, they'd nursed his sister for years. Of course they would have regretted things or would have loved to have done things differently. And they'd spent most of his life concentrating on the child who was sick, so maybe they didn't even know how to handle the child who was never ill. Maybe his health was nature's way of giving them a helping hand, as they needed to give all their light to Amber. Well, he thought, he was going to give as much of his light to them as he could. Maybe that's what he was there to do.

His thoughts took him to sleep in the back of the car and he slept till morning.

It was still dark when his grandma woke him and reminded him in sense to be ever so quiet.

They both crept downstairs. Bramble was in the back porch asleep on her dirty blankets, still literally in the doghouse after her muck-fest of the day before. She half-woke as they went past and Grandma spoke to her in sense and urged her to be quiet and go back to sleep. Her little docked tail was drumming rapidly on the floor as they left her and gently closed the door behind them.

Wrapped in her Harris tweed cape, Grandma was soon going great guns along the little path they'd made on their walks to the lake. Dill was skipping along behind her, full of excitement.

Just as at the spring gathering the landscape was moving with animals of all kinds. Low-flying birds like owls and harriers floated graciously over the dells, while flocks of geese flew higher. Dill could see the Brabbits all running and bouncing in formation like a military exercise being led by their mother, who was making her way through the dells like the expert she was. The sight of his friends made him light up inside and he picked up his own pace, overtaking his grandma on the path.

'Look, it's Grandma Vi and the boy!' a small deer was calling out to Gisela.

'Hi, Dill,' Gisela called. 'Hi, Grandma Vi.'

Grandma waved her stick in a friendly gesture. It was clear that all eyes and sense were on them as they hurried to the gathering.

The entire area around the shrunken lake was covered with the shadowy figures of the creatures of the dip 'n' dells. The heron from the spring gathering was bunched together with his wife and two young birds; the visiting flocks of wild geese took up much of the space at the head of the lake.

Grandma stopped by a rock and told Dill that this was where they would sit, which pleased him, as in the pre-dawn light he could just make out the Brabbit family huddled together on the other side of it.

A thin mist was lifting from the water, which was rippling with fish and frogs and other creatures coming up for a peek before diving back down with lots of plopping noises. The sound of the creatures settling into their places was like a slow chant as the first light began to shine from the east, to the left of the hill of the fairies. As the warmth of the first rays of sunshine touched the earth, the same fine white mist rose gently into the air and waved on Brigisha's last breeze like a flag of surrender to the pink summer sun that was now rising.

There was no fight or struggle between these goddesses. Brigisha had exhausted herself in causing a mighty hailstorm in the night and was now resting on the ground of the dells. As she lay there, the summer maiden stepped out of the sun and began to take form in the rising mist. She revealed herself as tall and elegant, slow and deliberate in every movement. She was a woman in her prime with silky red hair that ran all the way to her waist. Her gown shimmered with yellow, orange and golden beads and gemstones which sent out rainbow light in all directions. She was the goddess Lassaisha, and she was here to keep the dells creatures calm. She would nurture them in her term as governess of the sky.

The goddess drifted above the hill of the fairies and claimed her place officially in the sky, and at the foot of the hill the remaining mist parted and the iridescent white light of the Lord of the Dells shone through as he took his place to address all his creatures in this thin place at this thin time.

This was the one gathering of the year that included many new arrivals. As spring brought new life, so summer would teach them and help them to settle into their new world. The stag opened his speech with an address to the young, telling them the rules of the dells and the laws of nature.

'Creatures of the dip 'n' dells, I welcome you all to this special moment when life becomes thin and all of life can blend together as one.'

Dill was amazed, because he could feel the words in sense like never before. It was as if he was absorbing everything, and some of the teachings were reaching him on different levels. There were things he didn't understand now but understood that he would if he needed to. It was like storing knowledge for later, when it would be useful. He also felt that there was no need to try to work things out in his head; everything was just accepted by his light body.

The great speech the stag gave at this time each year was given to him by the summer goddess, who felt like a mother to all the newborn creatures and wanted them to feel protected in her time.

After the speech she granted wishes to those who had asked at the wish tree. When the time came to give them out, the place was filled with little lights that looked as if they had tiny people in them, just as at the other gatherings. This time little light people brought answers to those who had left wishes at the tree. They would just appear before them like a little light bubble, float there for a moment and then disappear into their hearts. It was awesome.

'Please, please, please' was all that could be felt around Dill's small party, as Dill and all of his friends hoped the goddess would grant his grandma's wish.

One moment thousands of little bubbles were shooting all over the lake and the next the wish-granting seemed to be over with a loud pop.

Instantly deflated, Dill, Jack and his two sisters all looked at Grandma and Mrs Brabbit. They hadn't flinched – in fact they both appeared to be preparing for something.

Then, out of nowhere, a pearl-like ball appeared in front of Grandma, and the stag said in his deep but quiet voice, 'After much consideration, a special wish has been granted to Violet Thornberry.'

The young ones filled with light again as they watched the pearl moving towards the centre of Grandma's body.

Then they heard the voice of the stag again: 'Do you accept the terms of this wish with grace and will you abide by those terms that you have agreed with the goddess herself?'

The little white ball hovered for a moment as Grandma took in the words of sense the great stag had given her, and Dill felt that something icy had touched his heart.

At the same time Mrs Brabbit nodded to Grandma in a show of support, as did Alice Otus, who had snuck in beside her.

Dill was wondering what all of this meant when he saw Grandma smile and say, 'With grace, my lord, and I will, my lord.'

She bowed to the stag and thanked him.

The creatures were silent, as like Dill and his friends they could feel something inside them they couldn't understand, but the Lord of the Dells looked directly at Grandma and said, 'Then it is settled.'

Chapter Fourteen
The Offering

The high that followed the summer gathering continued through the first two weeks of the new season. Dill and his young friends were happy playing in the safety of his garden in the blazing sunshine that was now bathing the land in warmth and light.

Swallows had built their nests under the eaves of Moon Cottage and Dill and his grandma loved to watch them swooping and soaring at great speeds, creating daring aerobatic manoeuvres that made for a thrilling air show.

Dill's parents were resting a lot in the garden, basking in the sun and allowing the season to heal some of the darkness that had haunted their minds for the past year.

Only Bramble looked uncomfortable in the heat. She took shelter anywhere the sun cast a shadow and spent most of the day with her long tongue hanging out of the side of her mouth.

As the weeks passed, Dill grew a little worried, because they were just a week away from the first anniversary of his sister's passing and he really didn't want to see his parents sad again, the way they'd been on Amber's birthday. He kept asking his grandma if she knew when her wish would be granted. He had a strong feeling that something good would happen for his parents the way it had for Jack's mum when her wish had been granted. But somehow he was also a bit scared.

His grandma would tell him that the fear was his doubt about whether the wish would work, and that it was perfectly natural to have doubts like that when you wanted something that much. She seemed very happy since the gathering, although Dill couldn't help but wonder what the stag had meant when he'd asked her if she understood the terms of the wish. Once again doubt crept in and he felt that there was something she was keeping from him.

But when Jack and the girls, who all felt as he did, asked their mum about it, she said exactly the same as his grandma. She also reminded her bunnies that the wish had been granted in the thin place and that there had been many great sense creatures there. If something had been hidden, wouldn't it have been felt?

The older women were probably right, Dill thought. Maybe the children all doubted because they hadn't the sense experience that the older ones had.

Jack's family came into the garden a lot now. His parents loved it when what they called the wild rabbits appeared. Dill's father even wanted to build a hutch to shelter them at night, but Mrs Brabbit asked Dill to talk him out of it. She hated the idea of being locked in a cage overnight.

His mother had become so fond of the Brabbits that she would bring them cabbage leaves and allow the 'wild bunnies' to take them off her hand. She had no idea that they were really coming to bring their light to her and her husband, or that it was what dells creatures did to heal each other.

Mrs Brabbit was now sitting by Grandma, who was on her rocking chair, which had become a permanent fixture in the garden. Grandma was pretending to feed her a cabbage leaf, but Dill knew they were talking sense. He couldn't quite read it, though. Mrs Brabbit was saying something that sounded like 'Alice says that everything is ready and that she has tested the route.'

'What did you say, Mummy, about a root?' Bunty Brabbit asked.

'Nothing – I said this cabbage would be good in a soup, ha, ha.'

Bunty's little nose crinkled like Bramble's, but she was crinkling out of confusion.

'Come on, children, let's enjoy the day,' Mrs Brabbit said, trying to draw their attention away from what she'd said.

Dill wasn't buying it. Again he felt a deep uncertainty run through him and he tried to work out why.

His thoughts were interrupted by Jack, who wanted him to get Bramble to come and chase him, as he knew how it made his father laugh. Whenever any of the Brabbits sensed Dill's parents go down, they were quick to help lift their mood.

Dill whistled to the panting dog who, no matter how tired, would always perk up at a chance to play.

Dill's father lifted his head the moment he heard the whistle, and like a shot Jack was off round the garden, followed by the brown and white hairy monster whose tail was wagging a 100 miles per hour.

Sure enough, Dill's father was doubled over with laughter. 'Ha, ha, ha, ha, ha!'

In the language of sense, both dog and rabbit could be heard laughing too.

The summer days were long and the mood around the cottage was good. Grandma passed most of the evenings reading her books before going for long late-night walks. Indoors, all three adults spent more time discussing things and Dill was pleased to hear it, as it felt as though there was some sort of life in the house again.

Sometimes he would feel the dark emptiness come in at night-time after his father and mother had raised their voices. Sense told him that the arguments always concerned his sister. It was crazy, because both his parents were right and both wrong, so no one could ever win. They seemed to be so out of keeping with their surroundings, Dill thought.

In the dells, nature got everything sorted because everything changed so much all the time, and all that was important was the place and time that they were in, but his parents kept dragging a past they couldn't change into every new season and somehow it didn't seem to belong.

He knew from Jack's family and from stories he had heard from some of the other animals and birds that many of them had suffered losses. Each of those families had felt pain and sadness, even anger, like his parents, but Mother Nature had taught them to move on. She had taught them to keep living in spite of their loss. She also taught that if you loved a family member or friend who had died, you were still connected through that love, because you weren't just the heavy hard body you thought you were, but an inner light, one that never went out, whether you were here or in Light Land.

Dill knew in his heart that there were lessons his parents could learn just by being in nature, even without his grandma's wish being granted. He had figured that death was part of life and it wasn't anything to do with right or wrong and it wasn't a punishment. He had learned this at the predators' pardon. He remembered the stag addressing the gathering and saying that the end of the hard life was natural, no matter how it ended, and that there was a reason for every death, just as there was a reason for every life.

He opened his eyes in the dimly lit bedroom and tried to adjust his focus. It was one of those hot sticky nights on which he found it difficult to sleep. Always when his mind was between sleeping and waking he would find himself going over things.

'Between sleeping and waking, that must be a thin time or something,' he said quietly to no one in particular.

Sometimes questions would surface then, and sometimes answers. Now, once again, he had a terrible foreboding about Grandma.

He turned on his side and tried to go to sleep. Maybe his brain was emptying out all the rubbish he had stored up over the weeks, that was all.

It was 21st May, the first anniversary of Amber's death, and both his parents were rushing anxiously around the kitchen.

'Tom, do get a move on. We only have an hour and I want to be there on time. You know you're always late.'

His mother was running a cloth over the breakfast table with one hand and running a brush through her hair with the other.

'I haven't finished polishing my shoes, Rose. Don't worry. We have plenty of time.'

'He's looking very smart today,' Dill thought. It was how he remembered his father looking in the old place, wearing a suit and tie and shiny shoes.

Dill's parents were going to the little chapel in Upper Dell to place some flowers there in memory of Amber, and his mother wanted to light a candle and say some prayers. They both wanted Dill to go with them, but his grandma had asked them if he could stay with her instead and give a little offering of wild flowers to his sister in the dells.

At first his father had protested, but Grandma had reminded him that Dill didn't need to see any more tears right now and she would make sure they made a lovely tribute to Amber there in the dells.

'Make sure that door's closed, Tom. The last time we went out you left it wide open – any animal could wander in.'

There was a distinct bang of the door.

'Dill, come and join us!' his grandma was calling.

In the garden with her were Mrs Brabbit, Alice Otus, the Brabbit children and even Bramble, all arranged in a circle. As Dill approached, she pointed to the spot where he should sit beside Jack.

'Thank the goddess we can get started,' Alice said. 'I should be in my bed, you know, Violet.'

Alice was nocturnal, which meant she slept in the daytime and did all her hunting and other owl stuff at night.

Grandma focused her mind on making good sense, a bit like clearing your throat to speak.

'Right, on the middle goddess day, that's 15th June to you and me, Dill, there is to be something special happening, and a part of the dells will become very thin for a moment. It's not an official thin time or place with a gathering and all the hoo-ha, but it will be thin all the same and I can use it to make my wish come true, and that is what is important.'

She looked around the group and it seemed that they were all on the same page so far.

'Bramble, off you go, girl.'

She gave the command and the dog was off and running, first round the edge of the garden and then over the wall. In commando style, she tore through bushes, bracken and thick mounds of heather, chasing everything within sight of Moon Cottage.

Alice took to the sky without instruction; she knew it was her job today to send anything in the sky off in another direction, clear of the house. Grandma was clearing the area in true military fashion; she wanted all sense creatures out of the way before she filled in the group with more details.

It was important that no sense animals spoiled her plans, or got in the way on the day they had to be carried out. The fact that it wouldn't be an official thin place or time meant that the predators could still hunt and she would have four rabbits working with her in the open in the middle of the day. She thought it wise not to put that about.

'OK, the next thing to know is that Dill's parents don't have much sense, so they are going to have to be tricked into coming to the thin place. Dill, that will be your job.'

He nodded and waited to be told what to do.

'No, I won't give out any instructions until nearer the time Dill. It's better that way. You young Brabbits will all be on lookout duty on the day, and Bramble and Alice will be watching over you both. Beryl and I have our own roles to play, and we'll tell you more about that when we feel that it's right.'

Of course Jack wanted to ask something. No sooner had the thought formed in his mind than the old lady was onto him.

'No, Jack, you will not tell Baggy, or any other animal friend you have. It is for that very reason that no more will be told to you at this time, do you understand?'

They did. The great thing about sense was how quickly things were understood.

Dill said, 'I feel better not knowing, Grandma, because I know I would let it out or ruin it somehow by accident. But I'll do whatever you want.'

The Brabbits all nodded their little heads in agreement.

'One thing,' Dill continued. 'We all knew that something was happening, but can you tell us how you and Mrs B. could talk sense without us knowing, Grandma?'

Mrs Brabbit piped up. 'The longer you talk sense, the less you have to use it to be understood, Dill – and if that doesn't make sense to you yet, then you aren't ready for it.'

Her little nose crinkled with each word of sense that left her mind.

'Well put, Beryl. I couldn't have put it better if I'd said...'

There was a pause and then both women burst out laughing.

The children had to laugh with them, and in so doing realised the meeting was over, as Alice landed on the roof of Moon Cottage just as Bramble leapt over the wall.

'We're all done here, Violet?'

Alice, it would seem, was anxious to get back to bed.

Grandma looked around the little gathering and said, 'Thanks, Alice, we're all done here. Speak soon.'

Alice Otus wasted no time in heading off towards her home in the darkest part of the old wood. The Brabbits stayed in the garden for a bit while Grandma and Dill prepared some things to take on their walk to pay tribute to his sister somewhere out in the dells.

Between the old wood and the hill of the fairies there was a stream that ran from the mountains beyond the dip 'n' dells into Lake Occasional. Grandma and Dill were walking beside it. For the first time she was taking him to what she called her special place.

They followed the stream from the nearest corner of the lake, just past the stones, for about 20 minutes until they reached a place beside the low wood. The land began to ascend here, and was rocky, with big green ferns and moss-covered boulders.

It was cool by the low wood and the sound of running water got louder the higher they climbed. Grandma's special place was a little waterfall that sat in the middle of this lightly wooded area. Dill could see in an instant why she loved it and why it was special to her.

'Moonwater Falls, I call it,' she said. 'It's not its real name, but I don't know that it has one, to be honest. I think my name suits it. Rowena showed it to me and I always found it was the place that called to me the most, especially when I needed strength, or to understand things. It always reminded me that life didn't need to be complicated. Do you know what I mean?'

Dill did. He'd been working out so much himself lately, and his grandma's sense was just confirming what he was learning.

'I think it's one of the most perfect places I've ever seen,' he said, 'and I know that Amber will love the fact that we're bringing her memories here today.'

Grandma smiled. It sounded as though he more than believed that a part of his sister would be there with them. But she had to know more.

'Have you ever thought that all the magical things that happen in the dells might be due to our imagination playing tricks on us and that one day you and I will wake up and everything will just have been a dream?'

'Yes, Grandma, and sometimes I've wondered if you've somehow created it for me, but that would be a bad thing and I know you could never hurt me. And anyway, far too many things have happened out here and I'm really glad they have.'

The old lady smiled at her grandson, pleased that even in such a magical world he still had a sense of grounding that kept him connected to his real world. She wanted to share more with him, but this was Amber's moment and they both felt it. So she pointed to a rock and motioned for Dill to join her there.

'This is where we should put the flowers,' she said. 'It's here that I say my deepest prayers for people and for the creatures of the dells, because I believe that if you give your prayers to the water it carries them away. And sometimes I write them on ribbons and tie them to the trees. That way the wind lifts them and takes them to higher places to be heard.'

Dill noticed frayed ribbons hanging from lots of the trees. Some had little messages that were legible, while others had faded with time.

'These are yours, Grandma? There are quite a lot.'

She slowly nodded in acknowledgement. 'Yes, Dill, there has been much to pray for recently.'

Dill liked the idea that his prayers could move. He put the wild flowers he had picked for his sister onto the rock and then threw them into the stream. He had the feeling that his prayers were alive because his flowers were travelling on the water and his thoughts were travelling on the wind. His prayers had left his head and were going on a journey.

Grandma took some ribbons and a felt-tipped pen from her pocket, handed them to Dill and told him he could put some prayers on the trees for the wind to carry.

He took them, moved to a separate rock and covered them with his arm, the way kids do when they are writing on an exam paper and don't want others looking over their shoulders. This made Grandma smile.

They sat in stillness while their silent prayers were sent out. The sense between them was strong, but didn't connect their minds at this perfect moment when their personal wishes, hopes and dreams were being set free.

Grandma let the painful memories of the last time she'd seen Amber in the hospital come back to her. It was a natural thing to happen and she allowed it. She could see herself talking to the child in a whisper and telling her that Grandpa was waiting for her in Light Land.

Then she remembered a dream she'd had a while after Amber's passing, when she'd gone to the cottage to prepare it for Tom and Rose. In the dream Amber and her grandpa had been standing together, bathed in light. They had looked so happy. It was this memory that she brought back to help her face the pain. She let it pass and soon memories of Amber as a healthy child of about seven or eight were playing in her mind. Amber had been a beautiful child, golden in nature, and she thanked the goddess for that.

Dill was remembering too. He was remembering being on a beach with Amber when he was seven and she was nine. That must have been when she began to get ill, because when they went home, his memories of her changed. She wasn't always in the house then because sometimes she was in hospital, and then the darkness came.

But, like his grandma, Dill allowed his memories to take their own course, and soon he was laughing about the time when Amber had used their mum's make-up to paint both their faces. How they had laughed that day.

In this magical place, the memories felt real to him. Amber's voice sounded like the sense voices he heard from Grandma, the Brabbits and the other creatures of the dells. It made him feel very close to his sister and that seemed to allow her to draw near to him too. Though he couldn't see her, he sensed her presence. She hadn't gone completely: as long as he could remember her, he could feel her there with him.

Sense kicked in again and Grandma announced, 'Right, now let's make an offering to the water goddess.'

'Who is the water goddess, Grandma?' Dill's big blue eyes widened in expectation.

Grandma didn't answer at first. Instead she went into her other pocket and took out a handful of seeds, as she'd done at the wish tree. She handed some to Dill and then said, 'That doesn't matter for now, but remember that if ever you go to a special place to pray, it is only fitting that you give something back to the higher elements that watch over that place. That way you won't drain special places of their powers and they will continue to assist those who come after you.'

'Special places… There are other thin places, aren't there, Grandma? I mean, it isn't only in the dip 'n' dells that time and places get thin, is it?'

She was glad that he'd asked this question. It was good to see him exercise his mind.

'No, of course not, Dill. People have always been going to thin places.'

He wanted to ask what she meant, but didn't have to.

'Think about it,' she said. 'When people are stressed, they go to the seaside. There's a thin place, remember, where the water meets the land and sky. And when someone is sick, they get taken off to the countryside to recuperate. Why? Because it's a thin place and has a healing energy that cities and towns don't have. It's natural for people to look for a thin place when they are in trouble. They usually don't have the sense to know what the place really is, but instinct, which is the first element of sense, takes them there.'

'Do you think Mother Nature designed it like that so that people couldn't ruin her special places?'

'I think that the great Mother Nature in her wisdom knows exactly what she's doing when it comes to people; only thing is, *people* don't know what they're doing when it comes to people. Places like this are full of magic that has never changed. It's people who are changing – they're looking at the world through very serious eyes and forgetting that there's a magic in nature that can teach them and help them. So many people look to their intellect and things like philosophy and religion for answers, when so many answers are in the world around them!'

She paused briefly for breath.

'Nature speaks to us, Dill. You hear it because you listen to the voice inside you. Now think about this: that voice really came to life when Amber got sick and you began to ask yourself questions, didn't it?'

Dill nodded.

'Because your parents couldn't find answers themselves at that time, Mother Nature spoke to you and decided to help you to remove the darkness from your world and from that of your parents too.'

There was such a lot to take in, but Dill was absorbing it on some level.

'I get that,' he said, 'but if we're forgetting about the magic in nature, does that mean we're losing our light bodies, Grandma?'

'No, Dill, sometimes we forget we have them, that's all. Lately people have forgotten what makes them truly happy, and some don't learn it till they've lost it.'

She smiled rather sadly, and Dill knew that the lesson was over. He stood up, threw his offering of seeds into the running water and said, 'Thank you for everything, good and bad.'

His grandmother did the same, adding, 'And thank you for the time we had Amber in our lives.'

Grandmother and grandson stood for a few moments and watched the water flow and the ribbons blow, letting the elements take their prayers where they needed to go.

That night Dill's grandma cooked a meal for his parents and deliberately talked about Amber and all the good times they'd had with her. When it looked as though they were going to get sad she would bring out pictures of them all laughing and having fun, and the photos triggered more joyful memories.

Dill was very proud of the old lady that night. And as for his parents, it felt as if a corner had been turned, albeit a small one.

On the eve of the middle goddess day all of the dip 'n' dells was thick with anticipation, though no one really knew why apart from the few who had gathered by the standing stones.

'Something's going on down there, but I'll be blowed if I know what it is, Barry,' one of the oldest crows in the dells was saying to one of his younger chums on the treetop beside him.

'Listen, Harry, it's all they can talk about tonight. The evening breeze is full of it.'

Two crows named Larry and Garry arrived on the branches beside them.

'You two know what's going on out there?' asked Larry.

'No, but something is. I've just said the same thing to Barry,' said Harry.

The cawing was booming out around the trees now.

Down by the stones Grandma was starting the meeting in concentrated sense to divert her awareness away from the sound of the crows in the distance.

'As you know, there is a plan for tomorrow.'

The youngsters waited eagerly to hear what that would be, but Grandma killed their hopes instantly.

'Each of you will be given your role then. Tomorrow morning, Beryl will inform the bunnies in the privacy of their burrow and just before she does Bramble will sweep the area and bark loudly to keep all the other creatures at bay.'

Alice had come up with that, as it meant that she wouldn't have to be there at the crack of dawn to sweep the air. She knew that birds never flew very close to Bramble when she was barking loudly.

'The breeze is thick with questions tonight, Vi,' Mrs Brabbit commented. 'So, Alice, Bramble and I have tried to put out the word that there is to be a thin place at the centre of the old wood sometime tomorrow and that everyone will know when it's happening by looking at the sky. We thought that would draw everyone away.'

Grandma nodded contentedly. 'Great. That will hit the breeze sooner than you think.'

'It's already started to move through the ground creatures like wind through the grass.' Mrs Brabbit said, looking quite proud of herself. She sat up and fluffed herself up a little, a bit like her son did on occasion.

For a moment there was total silence. Even the crows were quiet now.

'Ah, the breeze has reached the rookery at last.' Alice shook her body and gave her own little display of feather fluffing to let everyone know that her part had been successful too.

Grandma was contented, but the children, especially Dill, wanted to know what their parts were, and the oldies knew it.

'Dill, tomorrow I will fill you in,' Grandma promised, 'and when I tell you it will all make sense. We really don't want any of you to think that we are being secretive for any other reason than to keep other sense creatures away from where we will be.'

Dill did understand, but he still felt a little left out. Again the old woman sensed this.

'Dill, listen to the fuss the crows were making just now because they could sense that something was happening. Please try to understand.'

All eyes were on Dill and he had an overwhelming feeling of being scrutinised by sense.

'OK, I get it, but are you sure, Grandma? Are you all sure that you know what you're doing and that we have a chance of making it work?'

The air around them became serious as they all sensed his trepidation. He didn't know why he felt so concerned. He really appreciated that his grandmother was trying to help and he trusted her, but he didn't trust the unknown, where darkness could set in and things could go wrong.

'Dill, a thin place will open tomorrow, we have no doubt of that,' Mrs Brabbit said in a softer tone.

'We have the assurance of the stag himself,' Alice piped up in her most authoritative voice, 'And that came straight from the goddess, so we are certain of it.'

'It's going to happen, Dill, trust us,' Grandma said firmly. 'All of you, please trust us, and in the morning you will know the plan.'

With that statement, she brought the meeting to an end.

Chapter Fifteen
A Thin Place

Thankfully for Dill, his grandma didn't wait until morning before telling him a little of the plan. As soon as they got to the back porch, she asked Bramble to sweep the garden so they could share sense.

'We will only have a short time tomorrow, Dill, that's why I need to share some of the plan with you tonight. Beryl and Alice know the whole plan and have been helping me to prepare, and good old Bramble has been so valuable. She also knows some of the strategy, but has played dumb with you and the Brabbits so well.'

Dill was amazed. 'I can't believe that Bramble knows things and hasn't told!'

His grandma told him that the thin place would be at the stones. He had already guessed as much. The time, she said, would be given to them the following day, possibly even at the last minute, because they were waiting for a natural phenomenon to occur.

The ruse about the old wood was important because so much of what was going to happen would depend on them not being interrupted or witnessed by others.

Dill couldn't wait to learn what was going to happen, but his grandma told him once again to trust her and that he would learn more the next day.

'Bramble!' she called.

The big dog came bounding back towards them, sensing that her shift was done for the night. She looked at them both with her long tongue hanging down as she panted, 'Nearly there, Grandma. Phew, I'm exhausted.'

Dill wasn't tired that night. He lay in bed going over things in his mind. At least he had some new information now. How secretive the oldies must have been to keep their plan from the other sense creatures of the dells over the past few months. They definitely had a level of sense that he needed to learn. He pictured them meeting by the old wood, probably near Alice's home. He imagined that would be a very dark place and not many creatures would live there. He wondered if the stag had met them there or if the goddess herself had appeared to them.

'Wow,' he whispered as he rolled onto his back and looked up at the ceiling.

He wondered about what the plan was and how it would help his parents. His first thought was that the goddess would appear and bring Amber from Light Land in a little light bubble. Then he wondered whether the stones would become alive like people and would huddle around his parents and blast them full of light so that they would have amazing sense and be able to speak to his sister. He liked that idea.

'How cool stone people would be,' he whispered to the empty room.

And how devious the old woman had been. All that stuff that Baggy the badger had told them he'd overheard!

'Oh my God, they planned that. It was another ruse.'

He spoke out loud again, more directly to the ceiling this time.

Then he stopped. This was mad. His mind was jumping from one thing to another and he was talking to a ceiling.

But what a lot of planning had been going on in order to help his mother and father. He couldn't help smiling at the ceiling when he thought of it.

He wondered about the prayers he'd left at the waterfall. Maybe the little light bubbles had come and taken them to the goddess.

Again he whispered, only this time much more quietly, 'Please take my prayers and make the plan work, whatever it is.'

Already his mind was jumping in a different direction. One of the most brilliant things about this plan was that they were going to carry it out on Grandma's birthday. He began to appreciate how things were coming together. The middle goddess day this year fell on that day and the sly old fox must have known that for ages. She must also have reckoned that Dill's parents would be in the cottage preparing a surprise for her. This meant that they would both be where she wanted them to be.

'Pretty good planning for an old woman,' he thought.

His breathing was becoming softer and his thinking was fading quietly away as though an invisible hand was turning down an invisible dial. So many nights lately this had happened to him – he had fallen asleep in mid-thought.

He slept well, even though Bramble wasn't beside him. She was snuggled up downstairs beside his grandma, snoring loudly and taking up most of the old lady's bed. Grandma had kept the dog with her as much as possible lately, as she didn't want Dill to try and get things out of her. She knew he didn't like being kept in the dark and she really didn't like keeping things from him either, but she knew that if he knew what she was planning, he would never go through with it.

She nudged the dog with her backside and found a more comfortable position in the bed. Brambled sighed and they both followed it into sleep.

It was sometime just after the first rays of light had touched the dip 'n' dells that images and feelings began to occupy Dill's mind once more. He was in a thin place, the one between sleeping and waking, the time when dreams become authentic and carry a deeper meaning.

In this dream he was asking someone he couldn't see, 'Will the stag be there? Will the sky light up like it did when the air went thin before? What will happen to my parents? Will they get better?'

Then images begin to appear. He wasn't in deep sleep anymore, as he could hear things in two worlds at the same time. There was a noise in his bedroom, but he was pulled back into his dream.

He was back in the past, looking at the wish tree and his grandma hanging the second ribbon on it and touching the trunk. Then he saw the waterfall and the flowers and seeds running down the stream. And then he saw Amber, dressed in white and wearing the flowers they'd given her in her curly blonde hair. She was speaking to him, only his pictures didn't have sound, so he could only watch her lips move. Then he remembered that he could use sense and her voice was clear: 'I'm coming, Dill. Don't worry. I'll see you soon.'

Then he saw his grandma and she was standing on top of a large stone with her hands outstretched. 'I'm coming, Amber. I won't let you down.'

Dill's body jerked, but he didn't wake.

The vision changed and there was Lassaisha, the summer goddess. Standing in the dells, she was a giant woman who could reach the sky with her hands. In fact, she did just that and started pulling dark threatening clouds apart as if she was opening a pair of curtains. There was a circle of white light in the dark sky, which got brighter and pulled Dill towards it. For a moment he felt happy, but then the goddess was gone and the sky was dark – darker than dark, it was an inky blackness. Through that darkness came a flash of brilliant light, a breathing sound, a damp heavy feeling on his face and a pressure on his chest. He felt as though he was suffocating. He opened his eyes and sucked in a deep breath.

'Ahhh…'

The pressure on his chest was Bramble, who was furiously licking his face as she pinned him to the bed in full-blown spaniel attack mode.

Dill laughed and the spaniel's tongue went straight into his mouth.

'Ooh, yuck!'

Pushing her off, Dill fell out of bed and rushed to the opened bedroom door, as he knew that his dog wanted him to get up and go out with her. She pushed passed him now and he heard a tremendous pummelling noise on the stairs like a drum-roll as she headed for the kitchen and then out into the garden to freedom.

The kitchen was empty, so Dill headed for the garden himself. There he saw his grandma, with a look of concern on her face.

'I told them not to go today, Dill, but they didn't listen to me. They said they'd be back by ten, and I really hope they are, or nothing will work.'

She paced back and forth as Bramble began to run around barking like a mad thing. Anything within sense range scarpered for fear that she'd gone crazy.

'Quick, come into the kitchen with me and I'll go over things with you. Oh my, I do hope they come home on time, Dill.'

His grandma was definitely nervous, Dill thought as they sat at the table. He looked at the clock on the kitchen wall and saw that it was only just after seven. There didn't seem to be any need for all this fuss.

Meanwhile his grandma was straining her ear to the garden she'd just come from.

'OK, nothing out there. Right, Dill, here's how it's going to work – well, only if they get back, that is.'

Dill reached over and put his hand on top of hers. 'They will, Grandma. I can feel it.'

Slowly she began to relax a little and reveal her plans to him.

'The outline of the plan is this. You will be just behind the garden wall and the Brabbit children will hide in three separate burrows their mother has already dug for them, each positioned an equal distance along the path that runs from here to the stones. Are you with me, Dill?'

She was looking at him quite sternly; she wanted to be sure he understood what was going to happen.

'Yeah, I can see all of this. Carry on.'

'The Brabbit children will all be in sense range of one another and of Bramble, who will tell you when we've begun by barking one loud bark.'

Dill was trying to work it out. 'So, you start whatever you're doing at the stones, then each Brabbit sends out a sense signal along the path in turn and eventually this alerts Bramble, who barks to let me know that I should do my bit?'

'Yes, and your bit will be to cause high drama, Dill. I want you to be so convincing that both your parents come running to the stones to see what's wrong.'

'What will be wrong, Grandma?'

'Oh, nothing really. I'll have fallen on the ground, that's all. Don't worry, I'll be pretending, you daft bat. But I need you to keep up the pretence and really act as if I'm hurt, Dill. That will bring your parents to the stones.'

'OK, but didn't you tell us that this wouldn't be an official thin place and that predators would still be able to hunt? So, won't the Brabbits be in real danger?'

'Yes, but Bramble will keep her eye on the bunnies on the ground and Alice will have the air. She'll also be looking after Beryl at the stones when I go down.'

Mrs Brabbit was talking to her children at the same time and giving them their instructions.

'But what if there are foxes or hawks, Mummy?' Droopsy was saying.

'Listen to that dog out there – she'll be watching over you. We've checked the distance from one burrow to the next and Bramble can sweep them all in seconds.'

She sounded quite confident and her children could feel it. But Jack was a little annoyed that he wasn't able to do his mother's part at the stones. Even though he didn't know what that was entirely, he thought he could have learned it.

'Why can't we come to see the thin place?'

'Jack,' his mother said wearily, 'just try to go along with us on this.'

'OK,' Dill said, 'what about Mum and Dad? What's going to happen when we get them to the stones?'

'Well – look, maybe it's best if I begin at the stones and work that way.'

Grandma explained that first of all, she, Alice and Mrs Brabbit would get the sign that the thin place was opening. Dill wanted to know more about this, but she shushed him and carried on with her outline. The place would remain thin for no more than four minutes, so they had to be bang on time with everything. She was to position her body on the ground at the foot of the big moon stone and make it look like she'd fallen. Then Alice, who would be on the tree directly behind the stones, would give an unearthly screech, which would alert the first of the Brabbit girls, who would be lying in wait in her secret burrow. She would send out a heightened sense of alarm to her sister in the next burrow who would then send it on to Jack, who would alert Bramble to bark her loudest bark.

Dill was now in the flow. This would be when he did his dramatic act and screamed the place down for both his parents.

His grandma was most definite on this point. 'Don't come with just one, or nothing will work, Dill.'

'OK, OK, I've got it. And where will Mrs Brabbit be?'

'She will wait by the little healing stone at the foot of the seeing stone. You'll know why when everything gets going.

Dill made no attempt to ask any more. He was content to let his grandmother take him on her journey. When his parents reached the stones with him they would see her and go to help her, and if their timing was right it would be exactly the moment when the place became thin.

He was straining, but he could almost see it. He gave a nod and allowed his grandmother to continue.

'Don't worry, Dill, we've gone over everything 100 times and we've tested all the times to be sure that the children aren't in danger.'

'OK, just say all of this is to work and Mum and Dad do whatever they're supposed to. What will happen next?'

'Yes, good job you mentioned that. The next thing is, you will get onto the small healing stone at the foot of the moon stone behind me. You know the one I mean, the second healing stone. This is very important, Dill.'

She was looking directly into his eyes and he knew by that look how important it was.

'Can I ask why?'

'I'd rather you didn't, Dill. You will know when it happens.'

He was getting quite used to this by now and was about to speak again when his grandma began to talk in a way that felt that the words were coming straight from her heart. "Dill, I know that I have been keeping secrets from you and you know how I've always tried to be honest about everything. The only true thing I can reveal to you now is that I am honestly not sure what the outcome will be. I trust this place and the pact Ive made with nature; so I think I am asking you to trust me now and and have faith in what I'm doing, and with all your heart hope that it all turns out right.

Dill could only wonder what was to take place. It was strange, because even when he tried to imagine this thin place, nothing came into his mind except darkness. It kind of disturbed him.

'Grandma, have you got any idea what it will look like, this thin place?'

She shook her head slowly from side to side. 'I don't, Dill – well, maybe a little. The sky will definitely change just before it happens, of that I'm certain.'

Dill got a picture in his mind of the sky becoming dark with clouds. That was like something he'd seen before, but he couldn't for the life of him remember when.

'Grandma, this strange thin place, have you talked about it before with me, because something tells me I know about it, but it just escapes my mind at the moment.'

She got up from the table, her hand across her mouth; she was biting the inside of her cheek. But she turned to the window and spoke quite nonchalantly.

'Now, what we really need is for the goddess to clear the sky so we can watch for the eclipse.'

'Eclipse, Grandma, is that what we're waiting for?'

Dill remembered the big book of astronomy he'd found in her room and the conversation they'd had on their walk to the wish tree about the moon stone becoming active during a solar eclipse and how rare it was. And then he knew where he'd seen it before.

'Grandma, I've seen it already.'

'What have you seen?'

'I've seen this day, this whole day, in a dream.'

He tried to remember it, but it was quite fragmented, the way dreams are when people try to force them back into their memory.

'The sky is going to open, Grandma, and there is something to do with Amber at the stones. I've seen it and I've felt it.'

The older lady looked at her grandson for a moment. She was sensing what he'd seen, and though it was just a morsel of a dream, it lifted her.

'OK, let's get ready for the day. You're right, your parents will be back in time and all will be well.'

Her nerves had gone and the atmosphere lifted in the kitchen as Bramble returned from her mission, looking for a treat for her efforts.

At exactly 10.30 Dill's parents returned to Moon Cottage carrying bags which he knew were gifts for Grandma and food for her birthday dinner.

'Mum, why don't you take Dill and the dog for a long walk today?' his mother suggested. 'It said on the radio that there's to be an eclipse – he'd love to see that.'

His father was on his knees, trying to discreetly put food into the cupboards in front of him. 'I might want to have a look at that phenomenon myself, Violet.'

'Yes, I've heard about it,' Grandma said, 'and I will take Dill out to see it. I think we might head down to the stones. You get a good view of the sky there.'

'Mmm...'

Both Dill's parents mumbled something at the same time as they tried to hide presents and food.

His father stood up and turned to Grandma. 'Oh, I meant to tell you, I think we have an owl nesting in the shed at the side of the house.'

'Really?' she replied innocently. 'Are you sure, Tom? It's a bit late for the nesting season. When did you see it?'

'I saw it too, Mum,' Dill's mother chimed in. 'It went into the shed through that little hole under the roof, and we both saw it this morning.'

'How interesting. Dill, we must investigate.'

Dill had already worked out who this owl was and it didn't take long to deduce that she was camping there overnight, or day in her case, to be on time for the mission.

'Yes, let's, Grandma.'

Alice Otis was sitting on a shelf in the dark shed with her eyes closed tight. It was quite a comfortable place to have a nap in the daytime, she thought. She was happier to do this than fly out from the old wood in daylight, which would have alerted many of the other creatures to the fact that something was going on. Alice was organised and wanted to make sure that all the gang were in place when the time came to move. She was a stickler for precision.

She had never actually experienced an eclipse in her lifetime and she was a bit excited about it, but she was sad too. Grandma Vi, had become her friend and she felt that the sacrifice she was making was too much. Her mind took her back to the meeting she'd had with the stag by the wish tree before Lassaisha had come.

'Are you sure that the goddess in her wisdom and compassion will not accept anything else, my lord?'

The memory of his gentle eyes was so vivid.

'Those are the only terms she will accept.'

She could hear him now as clearly as she had on the night they'd met, and it was his last statement that stayed with her.

'Remember, Alice, under the law of nature, nothing is for nothing.'

Her eyes opened slowly as she became aware of the dog barking.

'Oh, there you are, Violet. Well, I've checked your timing and it's perfect, and we've done the dummy run in the burrows, Mrs B. and I, and they're all well within range. Bramble has timed the run at human pace and it gives three to four minutes for you to get into position.'

Standing in the shed next to his grandmother, Dill felt thrilled to be part of the exercise. Now that they were getting put through their paces it felt real. And how wonderful it would be if Grandma's wish came true and it really helped his parents.

Leaving Alice to get some more shuteye before things got under way, the two of them walked back into the garden. Grandma kept looking skywards, but now felt that things would be OK. The clouds where still there, but they were moving now and shards of sunlight were breaking through, forming great pillars of light across the landscape. It would be a clear day. They would see the eclipse.

Dill went back into the house to see what was going on and found his father reading the newspaper he'd got in town and his mother back on edge.

'I thought you were going out for the day with your grandmother,' she snapped.

'Don't take it out on him, he's just walked in, Rose.'

His father got up with his paper and walked towards the hall. Dill knew that he was going to his office to get some peace.

They had seemed too good this morning, he thought, but then again, they'd got good at hiding their feelings.

Maybe by tomorrow things would have changed.

It was just approaching midday when the clouds finally tore apart and sunlight flooded the dip 'n' dells.

When the sun burst through so did the sound of the breeze. Animals and birds from all over the place were sensing about the old wood and the unusual thin place that was going to open up there.

Grandma didn't mind winding some of them up. 'I'll be there as soon as the sky turns dark, Fred,' she was telling a skylark who was in the grass by the garden wall. 'They say it's going to be better than anything we've ever seen before.'

Fred seemed convinced, because as soon as he took to the sky he let it rip into the breeze and before long the air was thick with sense.

The atmosphere was also becoming thick, and for the first time that day Grandma could see the golden sun and sparkling white moon sitting side by side in the open blue sky. She knew that the thick atmosphere would soon become thin and wanted to get things started. Dill and Bramble could feel it too and just at that moment Mrs Brabbit popped her head out of Dill's den.

'Think it's almost time.'

There was a ghostly hush around them as every other living creature was heading to the old wood. They would see the sky turn dark there and it would create a thin time, but only at the stones would there be a thin time and a thin place.

Grandma and the Brabbits set off together over the garden wall. Bramble walked ahead of them along the path, sniffing furiously to make certain that there were no predators near the burrows.

Alice and Dill were at the entrance to the shed. Alice wanted to wait until the last minute to take her place, as she didn't want to be in the daylight any longer than she had to.

Dill suddenly remembered that he hadn't wished his grandmother happy birthday and it bothered him.

'Don't worry, Dill, I'll tell her,' Alice said in a gentler tone than he'd experienced in her sense before.

Everyone was taking their places. Dill's thoughts were with the little Brabbits in their little burrows. He was sorry he hadn't been able to speak to Jack and his sisters that morning. Bramble stationed herself opposite Jacks burrow; from there she could easily be heard by Dill and watch over the three Brabbits.

Dill climbed over the wall and walked a little distance down the path. Alice swooped past him, heading towards the stones.

The light was now changing and it looked as though the moon was touching the side of the sun.

'We're all set, girls,' Alice said to Grandma and Mrs Brabbit, with her usual wink.

Grandma turned to Mrs Brabbit, who was on the healing stone by the seeing stone, and they looked at each other for a moment.

'Is this it, Vi?'

Grandma didn't answer, she just nodded and looked up to Alice for approval. The owl nodded back from her branch.

'Thanks, Alice, for everything you have done.'

No words came back but a strong feeling of support was sent out in a good sense type of way.

It was Grandma who spoke again. 'I've got to see this through and you both know why.' She turned to Mrs Brabbit. 'Beryl, none of us know how my part will end, but I know you will look after my boy, won't you?'

'We both will,' Alice said, and now both her eyes winked at the same time and Grandma could feel emotions building. 'Oh, he wanted me to tell you happy birthday.'

Grandma breathed deeply and stood up straight as she looked up and realised that it could be the last time she would see the sky above the dip 'n' dells through human eyes.

The Lord of the Dells had told her that when the moon covered the sun on the middle goddess day the stones would become active and thin. He had also said that when that happened, if a person who had made a wish sacrificed a part of themselves out of love for another person, they could make their wish come true.

She had wished that her daughter's family might be allowed to see their daughter, Amber, one more time and hold her, so that they would get their light back for the sake of their son, who had been forgotten in their grief. These were non-sense creatures, so it was a lot to ask. For something this extreme to be given by nature, something just as extreme had to be offered in return.

So she had decided to sacrifice herself by throwing hers body off the moon stone. That should be enough to open up the thin time to non-sense creatures like her daughter and son-in-law.

The owl and rabbit wished they could have found another way to make this happen. But Violet Thornberry had her mind made up. She had planned everything down to the last detail and she knew that what she was doing would heal all of her family's hearts.

The moon had covered three-quarters of the sun and it was becoming very dark in the dells when Alice Otus let out the loudest screech she had ever made. Bunty Brabbit heard it and sent out her most powerful sense of urgency, which Droopsy Brabbit echoed to Jack Brabbit, who passed it on to Bramble. The dog gave one loud bark, which told Dill that it was his turn to act.

Flying over the garden wall, he let out a high-pitched scream that made his mother drop the plates she was carrying. He tore in through the back door of Moon Cottage.

'Mum! Dad! Help, it's Grandma! Please come quickly!'

He was crying as his father shot into the kitchen, and even before his parents could ask what was happening, he had turned and was back out of the door.

'Dill, wait,' his mother called, but he was half over the wall, with just a quick look behind him to check that they were following.

Back at the stones, Grandma had kissed her little rabbit friend on the end of her nose and thanked her before pulling herself up onto the big moon stone. She stood as tall as her body would allow on the large rock and concentrated on her light body. She knew that if she just thought of that, any pain from the fall would go quickly. She wasn't afraid of dying. It would mean that she would be in Light Land with her husband and her granddaughter and many others she had loved.

Bramble's barks were getting louder now and she knew there was just enough time to make the offering. She wanted it to be over before her family arrived. She didn't ever want them to know what she had done and she hoped that Dill would believe Mrs Brabbit when she told him that she really did have an accident, it would be the only time she really held the truth from him, but for the sake of the rest of his life she was offering herself for him.

The moon had now completely covered the sun. Only a thin ring of golden white light was shining out from behind it. The sky was dark, and the moon was dark too. Sun, moon and Earth were in complete conjunction. It was time.

Speaking out loud in a powerful voice that came from her heart, Violet Thornberry said: 'I offer myself in order for my family to be free of their darkness and pain. I do this with all my heart, which is filled with love for them.'

Gently, she rocked backwards and fell, with nothing in her heart but love and the promise of light.

Dill's father was first on the scene and his mother was two seconds behind, with Dill at her back. He remembered that he had to get onto the healing boulder at the foot of the moon stone and he did that straightaway.

'Grandma's pulling the greatest act ever,' he thought, as he looked at her motionless figure on the ground.

'Violet, can you hear me? Please tell me you can hear me,' his father was saying. 'She's unconscious, Rose.'

'Mum, Mum,' his mother cried, but the old lady didn't stir. Dill smiled at how convincing she was.

Above him was a ring of light, just as there had been in his dream. Shafts of that light shone down on the stones and in them he saw the face of the summer goddess, Lassaisha, looking calm and serene.

Then there was a great flash and all the stones began to light up from within.

Suddenly everything was calm and his parents weren't fussing over Grandma anymore but looking in his direction.

Turning his head, he saw Amber. Just as in the dream, she was wearing a long white gown and had beautiful flowers in her hair. She was bathed in light and standing on the moon stone behind him.

Then she stepped down on invisible stairs, as if she was walking on air, and touched her parents' hands.

They both became rigid with shock, for the touch was real.

Amber gently parted her lips and spoke. 'I had to come and tell you that I'm alright. I'm well now and free of the body that caused us all so much pain.'

Her words were making Dill's body vibrate, and he somehow knew that his grandma had put him on that stone so that Amber could use his sense to communicate from Light Land.

She looked at her mother and said, 'I'm so glad to have been your daughter and I want you to know that I will always be.'

She placed her hand on her mother's stomach and the dark boulder that Dill had seen earlier was visible again.

'There is a light in here,' Amber continued, 'and you have to allow it to shine again or my life and death will have been for nothing.'

Nothing happened for a moment, then golden light was breaking through the boulder like lava bursting out of a volcano.

Amber smiled and took her hand away.

Tears were running down her mother's cheeks. She couldn't seem to speak, but she wanted to tell Amber how much she missed her.

'I know, Mother,' her daughter replied. 'I can feel your pain, and sometimes your anger, and I have come to take it away with me.'

Dill watched the yellow light pouring out of the dark mass at the centre of his mother's stomach. Shafts of white light were beginning to shoot out of it too. It was amazing.

Amber looked into her father's eyes and told him, 'I love you so, so much and I need you to know that our bond will never break. It's forever, Daddy.'

Brilliant white light was now moving around the stones, sparkling like electricity.

Amber continued to speak to her father. 'I have come to ask your heart to let me go. The body you carry is dead, but I am still alive in your heart if you let the old me go.'

She placed her hands on his hands and then put them all on his chest.

'Feel my touch,' she said. 'I'm real and I'm well, and I love you and need you to release your anger, Father. Let the old me go.'

The words fell into the crevice that Dill had seen before and burst into light. His father's body was physically shaking like the flickering white light around the stones, and a huge lump moved up into his throat as he tried to say something to his daughter.

'I love you, sweetheart.' The words came from his heart.

The girl beamed a smile and addressed both her parents.

'The grief you have been feeling hasn't been about my death, but my life,' she said. 'You had to watch me suffer so much. Now, you should rejoice at my freedom.'

She opened her arms and embraced her parents, drawing them all together in a giant hug.

Dill was still watching from the stone, but his sister hadn't forgotten him.

'Look after Dill,' she told her parents. 'He is gentle and loving and kind. He is a special child and he needs you both to see him and hear him and allow him to grow naturally. And know that I will always watch over him.'

Dill could feel her words in sense and also feel tears running down his face as he answered, 'I know you will too.'

She turned to him and smiled.

'Call for me in any time of trouble, Dill, and I will be by your side. And know that I will be able to come to you in dreamtime and at thin times. Kiss Bramble for me and please try to save Grandma – she needs you all right now.'

There was a bang and a flash and she was gone.

'Quick!' Mrs Brabbit sent out a note of panic to Dill. 'Grab Grandma's ankle but stay on the stone.'

'What?'

He had no idea why, but he immediately obeyed.

At the same moment Mrs B. reached out with her front paw to touch her friend's head, and Alice Otus, who was now perched on the other healing stone of the moon stone, extended her wing to touch the unconscious woman's hand.

Light shot from the stones through all of them and into the body of the old lady. Its power was like nothing Dill had ever experienced before. It made his grandma's body spasm as if she'd been given an electric shock, but still she didn't wake.

Then light began to pour down on them from above. The moon had moved away from the sun. The thin time was over.

Dill's parents turned to help Grandma.

Alice flew onto the seeing stone above Mrs Brabbit, who was now also lying motionless.

Dill was telling his grandma to wake up and stop pretending. 'It's over, Grandma, come on.' But his sense shook inside him and he felt drained of power. Why wouldn't his grandma wake up?

Dill and Mrs Brabbit were sitting in Grandma's special place. They had made an offering of flowers to the water goddess, and Dill was now tying prayer ribbons onto the trees. Mrs Brabbit was showing him the tree that his grandma liked best.

They walked back through the dells and then past the stones in silence.

Suddenly Dill asked, 'What happened to all the Brabbits after the eclipse?'

Things had got so out of control that day that he hadn't even asked if they'd all got back safely.

'Bunty and Droopsy were OK,' Mrs Brabbit said, 'but there was a right old scuffle at Jack's burrow when Jonnie Fox found him and tried to drag him out.'

'Oh no!' Dill was shocked to think that his friend had been attacked.

'Is he OK?'

Mrs Brabbit began to laugh. 'He was a little shaken that day, but he's fine now. It was Bramble who was the real hero, of course.'

'Bramble?'

Dill couldn't understand why he hadn't heard anything about this before. Then he remembered.

'Yes, she appeared out of nowhere and shook old Jonnie by the neck like an old cabbage. Gave him a right old fright, she did, but she saved my Jack's life that day.'

Mrs Brabbit smiled.

'Still, she'll be up on a charge of assault at the next thin place.'

'No way!'

'Never mind, Dill. Alice is taking her case, so we have great hopes for her.'

As they reached the garden, Dill saw Alice herself perched on the wall. He smiled and said, 'It's good to see you, Mrs Otis.'

Alice winked her left eye at him and told him, 'Never mind all that, just hurry up and get in here, boy.'

Grandma was sitting in the garden in her rocking chair with both feet up on a stool in front of her and an arm and a leg in plaster.

'Did you send all my prayers, Dill?'

He nodded and gave her his biggest smile.

'Oh, you are a good boy.'

Dill was so pleased to see her. He'd been pleased to see her every day since they'd almost lost her at the eclipse.

The Brabbits, too, were bouncing around the garden with joy.

'Great to see you again, Dill!' Jack stopped bouncing for a moment to speak to him. 'Hey, what a crazy time, eh?'

'"Crazy" is the right word, Jack, but all is well now.'

Bramble had just noticed him and was running towards him too. She was covered in muck from the bog, but Dill didn't care. As he bent forward to hug her and kiss her face, she responded by giving a half-crinkle, which made everyone laugh.

Things were becoming normal, Dill thought. Well, normal if you lived in the dip 'n' dells, that is.

For almost three weeks he had been away living in a little hotel on the edge of the city, spending most of his days and evenings in the hospital pouring all his energy into making his grandma better. Poor Bramble had had to live in a kennel all that time and Dill had hated the thought of his beloved dog not having her freedom.

Something else had happened that did please him, though. During the time they spent away from Moon Cottage his parents seemed to reconnect in a way that had been missing for almost a year. They were very loving and attentive to one another, and he would often catch them holding each other. At night in the small hotel he would hear them talking through the thin walls until he went to sleep and in the mornings at breakfast they would always be holding hands and looking directly at each other when they spoke. Even his mother's nails were long and beautiful now.

Good things were happening and he was feeling much more relaxed now he didn't need to be so concerned about his mother and father. Even as he stood outside in the warm sunshine, he could hear them laughing and joking with each other in the kitchen. A light shone brightly from Moon Cottage, and it was coming from inside them as well as from the house.

'Come give me a hug and tell me how my special place is looking!' Grandma called out to him.

He held her tight and said, 'I really thought you were going to die, Grandma.'

'Thank the goddess for the second healing boulder, Dill,' came a voice from the fence.

As Dill turned to look at her, Alice gave him a wink.

It was the power of that boulder and the fact that Alice, Mrs Brabbit and Dill had all made a special connection that had really saved the old lady's life. The wise old stag had told the older ladies that if three of the healing stones could be connected when the moon stone was still active, new life would flow from it, that and love and friendship.

Dill kissed his grandma on the cheek and told her, 'I never want you to die.'

'Sweetheart,' she replied, 'I don't have time to die with all the work we have to do for Bramble's trial in the autumn. Anyway, what's all this about dying, Dill? We can't die for the life of us!'

Her laughter rang out around the garden.

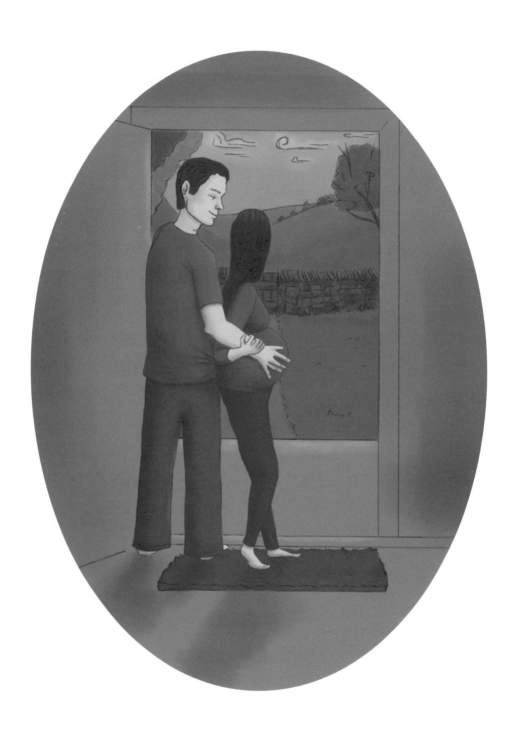

Epilogue

As the last of the summer warmth finally cooled and the sky above the dip 'n' dells began to grow dull and heavy, the summer goddess put all her efforts into creating an ending to her reign that would let the creatures she loved know that it was time for another change in their land. Her final sky was crimson and she went down with the sun above the low wood, where she rested a while in the evening calm.

Dill's mother stood at the back porch, filled with wonder.

'Look how magical the sunset is tonight. Everything is glowing,' she whispered as she tilted her head back to look into her husband's eyes.

His hands tightened around her waist and he gently kissed her neck.

'Yes, I see it, darling, and it is magic, but I think the glow coming from you is even more magical,' he answered, dropping his hands to the lower part of her stomach before tenderly kissing her mouth.

They stood for a moment smiling broadly, both staring ahead now at the last of the sunlight above the distant trees, neither aware that the red-brown clouds coming in from the east looked like a tall auburn-haired woman in the colours of autumn descending from the sky. And with her came a wind that raced through the trees.

Dill's parents both felt the chill, but they didn't move. They were ready to embrace the changes that lay ahead of them.